MYTHS OF EDUCATIONAL CHOICE

Myths of Educational Choice

Judith Pearson

PRAEGER

Westport, Connecticut
London

Library of Congress Cataloging-in-Publication Data

Pearson, Judith.
    Myths of educational choice / Judith Pearson.
        p. cm.
    Includes bibliographical references (p.   ) and index.
    ISBN 0–275–94169–8 (alk. paper)
    1. School, Choice of—United States.   I. Title.
LB1027.9.P43   1993
371'.01'0973—dc20   92–19594

British Library Cataloguing in Publication Data is available.

Copyright © 1993 by Judith Pearson

Library of Congress Catalog Card Number: 92–19594
ISBN: 0–275–94169–8

First published in 1993

Praeger Publishers, 88 Post Road West, Westport, CT 06881
An imprint of Greenwood Publishing Group, Inc.

Printed in the United States of America

The paper used in this book complies with the Permanent
Paper Standard issued by the National Information Standards
Organization (Z39.48–1984).

10 9 8 7 6 5 4 3 2 1

To our grandchildren,
in the hopes they will
still have choices.

Contents

Preface

The purpose of this project is to construct a few speed bumps in the path of the accelerating bandwagon of "choice." Speed bumps don't obstruct or stop a speeding vehicle; they slow it down for the sake of caution. They are intended to wake up the driver and avoid the kinds of tragedy that too much speed can cause. I believe that poorly conceived, hastily enacted programs of enrollment choice in education may do far more harm than good. The potential tragedies of this current reckless speed of change are lost opportunities for students (some groups more than others), weakened communities in rural America, and significant erosion of the basic structure of our democratic society. The issue of choice is controversial, and the debate is frequently heated. Both sides, however, agree on one thing: Choice will bring sweeping change. Common sense alone dictates that we take it slow, look both ways, and exercise prudence before crossing a major intersection in American education.

Given the speed at which choice legislation is being passed in the state legislatures and the enormous political pressure building nationwide with the consensus between the Bush administration and the private sector, the mere task of slowing the process is intimidating. In addition, I lack the customary credentials for engaging in a national policy debate of this magnitude. I am not on the staff of a prestigious institute or think tank, and I have no corporate, foundation, or organizational support for this project. This project is not part of an academic degree program and has no mentor's stamp of approval. This project is solely the result of my own experience and concerns.

However, I hope that my twenty-three years of experience as a public school educator, currently serving as a high school social studies teacher in the first "choice" state, will lend a unique, grass-roots credibility to my perspective. Most of the recent rhetoric on choice as a vehicle for reform comes from politicians, academicians, think tanks, corporations, or columnists. It's amazing so many people outside the public school system seem to know so much about what's wrong and how to fix it. I work every day with the students and parents who chose and those who chose not to choose. I have seen as many hurt as helped by choice. I have many unanswered questions and concerns about choice that surface as a result of my experience and understanding of public education.

My service in public education has included two years as a substitute and homebound teacher, working in four different school districts. I have taught thirteen years as a full-time secondary social studies teacher, working with students in grades seven through twelve, in school districts ranging in size from over 10,000 students K–12 to less than 600 students K–12. Four of those years were spent in an innovative, open/alternative school. I have a Specialist's degree in secondary school administration and hold Minnesota licensure for secondary principal and superintendent of schools. My service in educational administration includes seven years as principal (three at the middle school level and four at the high school level) and two years as superintendent of schools. During those two years, I led the district into a full, legal consolidation with the neighboring school district.

When local administrative opportunities were consolidated out of existence, I elected to bump back into the classroom, rather than pull up stakes and hit the road in order to stay in the fast lane, on the administrative career track. Our family and history and preferred lifestyle was in northern Minnesota. In addition to my professional service in education, I was elected to serve a three-year term as a school board director in my resident district (geographically, the largest district in Minnesota, and larger than Rhode Island or Delaware). Our two sons will graduate from this large but sparsely populated school district.

Both as a parent and as an educator, I have been concerned about the consequences of choice. I began questioning and raising these concerns when post-secondary options and open enrollment, two of the choice programs in Minnesota, were first proposed. I wrote position papers and submitted them to legislators and legislative committees, to no avail. Finally, in early 1989, I sent a hodgepodge of writing to the *Phi Delta Kappan* magazine as a response to a report on choice. The editor wrote back with an invitation to polish and publish, resulting in a short article in the June 1989 *Phi Delta Kappan*. For me, the article meant that I could put some of the professional anxiety about choice behind me. After all, I had done all that I could do to raise questions and concerns. However, the response to the article was not only surprising, but seemed somehow out of proportion.

I received many letters supporting my skepticism about choice. There were also interviews and invitations to speak, to discuss, and debate. The astounding part of this for me was the variety and scope of these contacts. I was called from class to answer phone calls from Texas, Florida, Kentucky, and the *New York Times*. I appeared on public television in the Twin Cities, at Penn State University and on the "MacNeil-Lehrer NewsHour." I was invited to testify before the Joint Education Committee of the Kentucky State Legislature.

As I participated in these discussions, debates, and pro/con forums, I became increasingly concerned about two things. The first and most obvious was: Why me? One short article, a mere classroom teacher from northern Minnesota—what's going on here? Where are the big names, the prominent titles, the significant affiliations? While I was asked to represent the skeptical perspective in these panels and interviews, the pro side included politicians, published professors, highly paid consultants, and "fellows" from institutes. I knew from the responses I received to the article that many prominent politicians, professors, and educators shared my concerns. Why were so few speaking out? What is it about the political atmosphere surrounding the issue of choice that is closing off debate? I find this very disturbing as the states and the nation introduce the most radical change ever to the institution of public education in America.

Equally frustrating was the conclusion that the time taken from family and school to travel and participate in these events was wasted. Even the ninety-minute format used in the Penn State program did not allow for depth or completion in exploring the issues related to choice. Too often the media time constraints resulted in panelists exchanging simplistic one-liners, generating more heat than light, providing more entertainment than enlightenment. The choice issues are too varied, complex, and important to receive adequate examination by television. It was this conclusion that prompted me to tackle this project. My goal is to describe as clearly and completely as possible the concerns and questions about the choice programs being proposed and implemented around the country. My objective is to cause sufficient pause in the minds and actions of the policymakers in education to ensure that choice—if, when, and where enacted—will be in all its consequences as American as "freedom of choice" sounds.

MYTHS OF EDUCATIONAL CHOICE

1

Choice and Crisis

Of course everyone supports the concept of freedom of choice. That expression is as American as "the Fourth of July." It is no surprise that opinion polls are showing increasing public support for the general idea of enrollment choice in education. It goes with, rather than against, the grain of American tradition. In a relatively short period of time it has become almost un-American to even suggest that parents should not be allowed to select the best school for their children. However, this simplistic groundswell of support for enrollment change in education does not reflect an appreciation of the depth and breadth of change rolling into our public schools on the bandwagon of choice. Traditional and very basic tenets about the role of public education in American society are shifting dramatically. If choice in education is suddenly so American, so automatically popular, why did it take so long? Why haven't we had it all along? Why now?

There seems to be a strong correlation between the growing popularity of choice and the general perception of crisis in the nation's public schools. This connection is evident in the 1991 Gallup Poll of the public's attitudes toward the public schools, in which only 21 percent of the people polled gave the nation's schools a grade of A or B, but 62 percent favored public school choice. It is interesting to note that in the same Gallup poll, people gave their local schools much higher grades than they gave the nation's schools. Furthermore, the public school parents polled expressed enormous confidence in the school their oldest children attend. In other words, "my public school is fine, but all the rest are failing." As Elam, Ross, and Gallup (1991: 54) said: "The most plausible explanation for these disparities is that the more firsthand knowledge one has about the public schools, the more favorable one's perception of them. In short, familiarity with the public schools breeds respect."

Is the widespread notion that our schools are failing based on knowledge and experience or on unquestioning acceptance of a decade-long, negative image portrayed in the media? The Gallup polls also show that the public's ratings of its local public schools have remained basically stable since 1984. This followed a low point in 1983, when the poll was conducted, "just after *A Nation at Risk* was released by the National Commission on Excellence in Education and was widely publicized by the media" (Elam 1990: 50). From "the rising tide of mediocrity" cited in *A Nation at Risk*, commissioned by the Reagan administration, to the October 1991 report released by the Bush administration's National Education Goals Panel, the typical headline reads, "U.S. students are at the bottom of the class." Generalized, across-the-board school-bashing is the fastest growing sport in America.

No wonder the general confidence in public schools is down and the pressure for reform is building. But is it reform or is it change for change's sake? How could anyone maintain positive attitudes in light of recent media coverage? This coverage includes national newspapers, news magazines, network news and CNN. Just how influential is the media in shaping public opinion? Space and time do not allow exploration of that issue here, but it is generally accepted that it helps elect presidents and determine the outcomes of war. Because the education "crisis" is the springboard for choice, let's examine that basic assumption more closely.

How do we determine if the public schools are really failing so miserably? If a student comes home with a report card filled with failures and incompletes, as Bush's National Education Goals Panel issued U.S. students in 1991, the parents go to school and ask questions. Who gave those grades and why? What were the grades based on? Who was the student graded against, compared with? What kinds of tests were given? It is interesting that while individual parents will not automatically accept the notion that their own child is a failure, collectively we seem to automatically accept failures and incompletes on the national report cards without asking the same basic questions.

Most of the negative reports on public education that receive such heavy media coverage have been based on test scores. Seldom in the media are these test scores ever questioned. An in-depth description of the limitations of educational testing could fill a library. However, all educators understand that there are limits; therefore, there are significant dangers in over-interpretation of the test scores of students. Test construction, administration, reliability, validity, the development of relevant and representative norms, the sampling methodology, and potential cultural bias implicit in the testing itself suggest some of the variables that can affect test results.

Example. In school A, all 150 eighth-grade students are given a standardized achievement test in reading, mathematics, and social studies. For administrative convenience, the test is administered over four days in all six of the eighth-grade geography classes. This involves three different geography teachers. There are no training sessions for these teachers. They are simply handed the materials and told to play the taped instructions and follow the manual. One teacher follows the manual to the letter, plays the tapes diligently and finishes in four days. The other two teachers dispense with the tapes because most students can read the instructions quicker on their own and the testing is completed in three days. It should be noted that in school A, where the test is administered in the social studies classes, the student population being tested includes all mainstreamed special education students.

In school B, the same tests in reading, mathematics, and social studies are administered to the 150 eighth-grade students. However, in school B, the testing is coordinated by the school counselor, who uses the English classes to give the test. The English teachers are instructed about the test and the testing environment in advance and the counselor assists in proctoring the testing. In school B, the special education students with learning disabilities in reading are not mainstreamed in the regular English classes. They receive their eighth-grade English instruction from a special education teacher according to their Individual Education Plan (IEPs) and are therefore not included in the test group.

When the average group scores are reported for schools A and B, school A scores significantly lower on most items. It should be obvious that comparing student achievement in reading, mathematics, and social studies in schools A and B based on the described testing programs would be ill-advised, inaccurate, and potentially dangerous, depending on the conclusions drawn and/or actions taken. Yet the temptation is there. After all, the tests and grade levels were the same, and the numbers, rankings, and percentages on the scoring printouts imply a precision that camouflages those variables that skewed the outcomes. In my experience as a teacher and administrator, the inconsistencies and discrepancies of educational testing described in the example are the rule, not the exception.

The 1991 report from the National Education Goals Panel headlined the fact that in 1988, American students scored substantially lower than students in three out of four other countries on an international assessment of science achievement given to thirteen-year-olds. In 1988, the report continues, American thirteen-year-olds scored lowest among students in five nations on an international mathematics test (Rothman 1991: 18). The five nations, ranked from first to last, include South Korea, Britain, Spain, Ireland, and the United States. Supposedly, the tests were the same, and the ages tested the same. What more could one possibly want to know before comparing, concluding, and acting on the basis of the test results?

Does each country's sample reflect its entire student population? Is the universe of students tested consistent from country to country? Is it possible that over 80 percent of U.S. students are being compared with only about 20 percent—the highest-achieving 20 percent—of European students attending upper secondary school? This is what happened when the International Association for the evaluation of Educational Achievement (IEA) conducted the first set of international comparisons in the 1960s and early 1970s (Rotberg, 1990: 296). Rotberg suggests similar problems exist with the 1988 math assessment, conducted by the International Assessment of Educational Progress (IAEP), which ranked U.S. thirteen-year-olds last in mathematics: "Because of the small sample size and the acknowledged methodological problems, this assessment was labeled a 'pilot'—although this label has not been reflected in public rhetoric about the results" (1990: 298). Perhaps we need to be skeptical of the "public rhetoric" as well as the test score analysis.

And what about those awkward declining Scholastic Aptitude Test (SAT) scores?

Example. In 1980, counselor A at South High School described the SAT to the junior class. He made his presentations in the advanced math and honors English classes, knowing that these were the students most likely to attend private or out-of-state colleges and universities. He also explained to the rest of the college-bound juniors that the most appropriate entrance exam for them was the American College Testing Program (ACT), which was required by the state college and university system. By 1990, new-hire counselor B (A has retired and is passionately tying trout flies) at South High School described the SAT to the entire junior class, stressing the importance of a college education and the need to take the SAT in order to keep all options open. In 1980, only 10 percent of the junior class took the SAT, while in 1990, over 30 percent of the junior class took the test. Predictably, the 1990 SAT average scores were significantly lower than the 1980 SAT scores for the juniors at South High School. When the local media headlined this dramatic decline, the school board scheduled an emergency session to consider corrective action. After all, it's the same test, same grade, same high school—what more do you need?

It seems that sampling problems might not be limited to international testing and comparisons. Isn't it also possible that the well-publicized decline in SAT scores is influenced by the larger number of students taking the test and attending college? Gerald Bracey suggests:

> To understand this point, recall that the standards on the SAT were set in 1941. . . . In 1941 an elite group of 10,654 mostly white, mostly male, mostly northeastern students, mostly headed for Ivy League and other prestigious private universities, sat down to take the SAT. During the 1989–90 school year, 1,025,523 students (about 42% of the entire senior class) paid for that privilege. (Bracey 1991: 108)

As Rotberg reports, even the relative rankings of states on average SAT scores are a reflection of the proportion of students who take the test: "The states with the highest proportions of students taking the SAT tend to have the lowest average SAT scores. Indeed, one way to increase a state's average SAT score would be to discourage students from applying to colleges that require the test" (Rotberg 1990: 297).

The concept of decline and crises in student achievement is further challenged in a study released by the National Assessment of Educational Progress (NAEP) in October 1991. In science and math, the study found that the proportion of students who could perform more complex problems increased substantially over the past two decades. The full study examined national trends in average achievement in science, mathematics, reading, and writing and concluded that student performance in 1990 was roughly at 1970 levels (Rothman 1991: 14). The term "average" may be significant. If these results are compared with retentivity rates over the same period of time, similar average scores might suggest an improvement over 1970 student performance if the number of students tested has increased.

In reality, educational test scores, despite the concreteness and exactness of the numbers, tell us very little precisely, and even then, it's only part of the story. Public schools in America play a much broader role in our society than just educating students to score better than South Korean students on math and science. Our students could spend more time in longer school days, longer school years or on mandatory homework, which might make them more competitive on narrow international assessments. But this additional time would have to come from the organized and productive extra- and co-curricular activities that teach skills and develop qualities not easily translated into measurable test scores.

The athletes who practice for hours every day and play their hearts out in competition are learning sacrifice, team work, leadership, and sportsmanship. When they lose a tough game but come back to play their best the next game, character scores high. The students winning parts in school plays, participating on debate teams, or playing in musical ensembles learn the responsibility of having others depend on them for every practice and performance. The students involved in student government know the challenge of leadership when they organize and lead others to transform ideas into real experiences. These activities build character and continue community traditions.

Before we reduce our evaluation of the American public school experience to the lowest common denominator of narrow, international test score comparisons, we'd better expand the equation to factor in all the variables. Perhaps other cultures provide the same wide range of learning experiences to their school children. Or perhaps these experiences are not important. Let's at least examine the whole story before we throw the baby out with the bathwater. Many thousands of American students are spending countless hours in these activities learning significant life skills and developing the kinds of character that just might be part of what makes America great. We are training future world leaders that need knowledge, but also need the skills and character to use that knowledge wisely. If leadership and character are difficult to quantify, does that mean they should be left out of consideration?

Could there be some good news buried in those test scores? Over the past few decades in American education, we have endeavored to broaden the base of opportunity and increase the participation in our public schools. From *Brown vs. the Board of Education* to 94–142, from Title VII to Head Start, we have succeeded in bringing more school-age children into better, more equitable schools and keeping them there longer than ever before (or perhaps anywhere else). It's far from perfect, as evidenced in Jonathan Kozol's *Savage Inequalities* (1991), and there's a long way to go—but why didn't someone warn us that these admirable efforts might temporarily result in some lower averages on test scores?

Reporting and interpreting educational test data is analogous to over-driving a car's headlights—tempting but dangerous. Comparing student achievement in school A and B from the first example is like comparing apples and walnuts. How about South Korea and the United States? No answers here, only the questions. Why aren't the questions ever asked or covered in the media?

Perhaps part of the explanation is the common criticism of the media that bad news makes better news. In addition, the popular media may be constrained by the complexity of the statistical analysis required to ask or report the rest of the story about test scores. Measurement concepts such as stanines, standard deviations, sampling, and statistical significance may be more than the media and the general public can deal with.

However, a controversy that surfaced in September 1991 suggests a less innocent explanation. The controversy began in early 1990 when the U.S. Department of Energy initiated an educational outreach program. The analysts at the Sandia National Laboratory in Albuquerque, New Mexico, began the project logically by reviewing existing research, interviewing educators, and conducting site visits to schools. The results of this analysis were summarized in an *Education Week* article, "Energy Department Report Questioning 'Crisis' in Education Sparks an Uproar" (Miller 1991: 31).

Based on existing data, the Sandia researchers found that U.S. high school completion rates, including equivalency diplomas, are improving and among the best in the world. They also found that the decline in college-entrance examination scores is due to a wider range of students taking the tests. When corrected for demographic changes over 20 years, no decline in scores is evident. In addition, American participation in higher education is the highest in the world. Findings also included the fact that while educational expenditures have increased over 20 years, "the increase has gone almost entirely to special education, and it is thus unfair to assert that increased funding has not improved the performance of students in general" (p. 32).

The findings are certainly intriguing, given the current public rhetoric and crisis mentality about education. The uproar over the findings is disturbing: "Some members of the research community charge that the Bush Administration is suppressing the report—which was prepared as part of an Energy Department education initiative—because it conflicts with its own rhetoric" (p. 1). That rhetoric is: "Look, we've spent all this money on education and the scores are still declining, so let's drop money and go to choice."

Concerning the study, "the Sandia researchers 'were told it would never see the light of day, that they had better be quiet,' one source said. 'I fear for their careers' " (p. 32). The article did report on one area of agreement between Sandia analysts and administration officials: Available education data are inadequate. The intrigue is that on the one hand, the administration finds existing data adequate to determine that our schools are failing and to justify systemwide, sweeping change, but just inadequate enough to discredit and bury a report that is counterproductive to its policy agenda.

In July 1991, one of the researchers and the director of Sandia's education effort testified before the House Subcommittee on Elementary, Secondary, and Vocational Education. "We knew it was only a matter of time before their chain was jerked," one Democratic committee aide said, "so we wanted to get them on the record while we could" (Miller 1991: 32). Why would the administration—or anyone, for that matter—want to suppress a study that concludes that American education may be satisfactory after all? Are test scores and data analyses being manipulated to serve political purposes? How does the general public detect this kind of manipulation when the data are so seemingly precise, so implicitly objective?

The intention here has been to raise doubts about the doubts. The belief that the public schools are failing is built primarily on negative media reports, which are based primarily on test scores. This belief is the central axle of the choice bandwagon. Apparently, test score information can be flawed by methodology and manipulation. The Sandia study concludes that policymakers and pundits who bemoan a systemwide crisis are both overstating and misstating the problem. "Unfortunately, much of the current reform agenda, though well intentioned, is misguided," one version of the report states. "Based on a 'crisis' mentality, many proposed reforms do not properly focus on actual problems" (p. 1). Is there or is there not a crisis in education? Who bears the burden of proof?

From another perspective, would a physician amputate the leg to remove an infected toe, surgically remove the spots to cure the measles, treat a hypochondriac with addictive drugs or use massive radiation to remove an unsightly mole? The mole is gone, but the patient died from adverse side effects. Similarly, with the current "crisis" in education, we need to check perceptions against reality, sort symptoms from causes, and ensure that the changes introduced don't do more harm than good. If inner city schools are failing, why "fix" the entire state? If property tax funding results in inequities and some schools failing, do we change the tax structure or the schools? If crack cocaine is destroying entire neighborhoods, how do we fix the neighborhood school? If individual students can't get oboe lessons or calculus or German in their local schools, do we let all students go to any school for any reason? What exactly are we fixing? Will there be adverse side effects, inadvertent consequences? Is choice a panacea or a Pandora's box?

Discussions about educational policy are frequently conducted in a cloud of jargon and overlapping issues. Choice is no exception. Before examining some basic questions and reservations about choice in succeeding chapters, it is useful to define the terminology and sort out the issues. "Reform" and "restructuring" are two terms commonly used in connection with choice. According to Webster, both terms involve change. Choice also involves change, but that's where the agreement ends. "Reform" means to correct, to improve by change, change for the better. The use of the term implies that something is wrong and in need of correction. Obviously, that's debatable. Whether at the state or national level, choice is across-the-board, systemwide change. Is the something that's wrong across-the-board, systemwide? Reform is defined as bringing improvement, something better. Choice will bring something better for some students, but not for all students. Choice may bring much less for many students and intensify existing inequities. Choice is change, but reform it is not.

What is restructuring? Anything one wants it to be! A survey of the professional journals in education suggests it is nothing more than a four-syllable word for change, a classic example of ambiguous jargon and equivocation. No one has a precise definition, but everyone uses it. The only certainty about the term is as a prerequisite for publication. Look at the titles: "Restructuring Through School Design," "Restructuring an Urban High School," "Initiating Restructuring at the School Site," "Restructuring Teacher Education," "Restructuring Education Through Technology," "Restructuring Personnel Selection: The Assessment Center Method," and "Restructuring Early Childhood Education" (Kappan Fall 1991 Fastback Series).

Although the term has "structure" in it, little or none of the rhetoric refers to the school buildings, which may indeed be in critical need of restructuring. Webster indicates the term means to change the makeup, organization, or pattern of something. As Walter Shapiro writes, "Make no mistake, a major part of the allure of Choice in the frugal '90s is that it promises a radical restructuring of American schools with a minimal investment of federal funds" (Shapiro 1991: 56). The only thing choice restructures is funding formulas. But will it make things better? What things, and for whom?

The concerns raised here began when the issue was simply choice, Minnesota-style, because that's all there was. The primary concern was not choice per se but interdistrict choice (between school districts) and the consequences of state aids following students in a relatively unrestricted choice program. Intradistrict choice (between schools within one district) and alternative programs within a district were never concerns, because the resources and responsibilities for equitable opportunities for all students remain with the district, within a single jurisdiction.

However, the field has expanded and the issues have multiplied with lightning speed. Minnesota's open enrollment was the first and was not fully implemented statewide until the 1990–91 school year. By 1991, Minnesota had added "charter" schools, ten other states had passed comprehensive, statewide, interdistrict choice plans and President Bush had made public funding of private schools a part of his America 2000 strategy. "Stateline" in the October 1991 *Phi Delta Kappan* is titled "The Vouchers are Coming!" (Pipho 1991b: 102), and a four-page advertisement by Chrysler Corporation in the October 21, 1991, *Time* magazine asks: "Do you agree: Students should receive government vouchers to pay for their tuition in any public or private school." With vouchers back on the front burner, consideration of choice must also include some attention to the ancient debate on the merits of public versus private education and the divisive church versus state issue.

During the 1990–91 school year, the Milwaukee schools began a choice plan that provided public money to follow students to private schools. This plan is being challenged in the courts on the question of separation of church and state. Unfortunately, whatever the courts decide, the real issues underlying the Milwaukee plan will be obscured. The Milwaukee plan was initiated because integration orders had failed to provide equitable and quality neighborhood schools in the inner city. Desegregation compliance brought large amounts of money to certain inner city magnet schools. White students came, but when local black students tried to enroll in their own neighborhoods, they were turned away because of numbers and compliance requirements. Choice was the last resort, but a resort that attracted an interesting coalition of political and private supporters who now had an acceptable way to avoid paying the bill to improve all inner city schools.

Brown vs. Board of Education made it into the law journals almost 40 years ago, but it still hasn't made it into the hearts and minds of black students. De facto segregation and white flight prevail. Just under 100 years ago, *Plessy vs. Ferguson* required that separate facilities at least be equal. As Jonathan Kozol describes in *Savage Inequalities* (1991), the schools are still separate and equality is a figment of a naive imagination. Still separate and still unequal, no progress. What choice did concerned black parents have but "choice"? But will choice Milwaukee-style reduce or increase the inequities that exist for all inner city children?

There is a crisis in education, but it's not nationwide and it's not found in test scores. It's found in the inner city and obscured by the issues of race and class. It is undoubtedly the most difficult, pervasive, and perverse problem in education and society in general. Is choice the answer? Certainly it will be for some of those who choose. But studies show most won't choose, and for them, it will only get worse. Isn't choice in this instance a cop-out, a simplistic, quick fix for what are otherwise complex and expensive problems to address? Let's not be naive in our consideration of the pros and cons of this policy debate. As we hear about the isolated success stories of some who chose, let's remember to ask about those who stayed. Since we know a little more about sampling, let's also remember to ask about all the numbers. How many stayed and made do with how much less?

The impacts of choice in an urban or inner city setting are significantly different from the impacts of choice in a rural or small town setting. The first involves issues of racial segregation, poverty, unemployment, health care and crack cocaine, to mention a few. The second involves issues of geography, sparse population, economies of scale, community, and the consolidation of schools. It would be helpful if the national debate would distinguish between the two. Although this project has its origin and primary involvement in the rural area or small town, greater (outside the Twin City metropolitan area) Minnesota setting, the choice plans are systemwide and thus require some attention to both rural and urban issues.

Examples were used in this chapter to illustrate problems with test score analysis. Similar examples will be used throughout this book to represent the experiences with choice. Most of the research for this project was done by interview, often with minors or with professionals who spoke off the record. In most instances, the examples reflect actual experience. Any hypothetical examples are identified as such. The most common evidence offered by the proponents of choice are single case examples, vignettes of heart-warming success stories. There are also stories of the heart-breaking failures of choice and of the consequences of choice that have reduced rather than expanded opportunities for many.

2

Choice and Minnesota

"Education was my passport out of poverty," wrote Minnesota's former Governor Rudy Perpich (Nathan 1989: 1).

> The Governor knew the value of education as he is the son of a coal miner who had little opportunity for formal education. The Governor himself would have been eligible for English as a second language classes had there been such programs when he was a child; Governor Perpich could not speak any English when he started school. (Randall and Geiger 1991: 147)

Randall and Geiger explain that Perpich keeps a list in his desk drawer of former teachers that he credits for giving him a "passport" from poverty. Presumably the list is to help remember. Perhaps he should have added to the list that his impoverished parents could not have afforded to transport him to the neighboring school district if he had chosen to go. He forgot that the quality of his education was totally dependent on the existence of a neighborhood public school!

Yet Governor Perpich was the prime mover in introducing choice into Minnesota schools and thus the probability that quality, public neighborhood schools will no longer be there as passports out for many rural and/or inner-city poor students. Why? This question is particularly significant because by all measures, Minnesota's schools consistently lead the nation. According to the U.S. Department of Education's revised Wall Chart (State Education Performance Chart, May 1990), Minnesota ranked first out of the fifty states with the highest high school graduation rate from 1982 to 1989. When combined with the other categorical comparisons, Minnesota's education performance would be the envy of at least forty-five to forty-eight of the other governors. This may explain why the 1990 Wall Chart will be the last, according to an official with the U.S. Department of Education. The governors don't like the comparisons and have complained to a newly sympathetic and politically sensitive secretary. For Governor Perpich, the question remains: Why fix what's working? Doesn't it challenge common sense to introduce the most sweeping, radical change ever to an educational system that leads the country?

Governor Perpich's oft-repeated explanation was his children's school experience in the Minneapolis-St. Paul metropolitan area. After his election to the State Legislature in the 1960s, his children found that their classes were mostly a review of material they had already learned in the Hibbing, Minnesota, schools. As he writes:

> But, when my wife and I talked with teachers and school administrators, we learned that we had no options for more challenging assignments or moving our children to another classroom or school. That is why I recommended in 1985 that we allow Minnesota families to select among various public schools" (Nathan 1989: 2).

Aside from questioning the wisdom of basing broad social policy on relatively narrow personal experience, one wonders whether it alone could have provided the energy and momentum necessary to push choice into law twenty years later. A more probable explanation is found in an examination of politics, pressure, and the private sector. Governor Perpich was defeated in a bid for a second term as governor in 1978. In the interim prior to his successful bid for re-election in 1982, he worked for Control Data Corporation. Control Data is a member of the Minnesota Business Partnership, an organization of the chief executive officers of the state's largest private employers. In 1983, the Minnesota Business Partnership commissioned a study of Minnesota's K–12 public school system. The study was done by BW Associates of Berkeley, California, and recommended increased choice for high school students. In 1986, Education Alternatives, a for-profit company spun-off from the multibillion-dollar Control Data, was formed with the vision of running a national chain of for-profit schools (Shapiro 1991: 59).

There is no intention of developing a conspiracy theory here. In fact, the Minnesota Business Partnership is quite explicit about its role in education policy. Its 1990–91 *Resource Book* explains:

> The Partnership was instrumental in persuading the Governor and Minnesota Legislature to adopt a series of education "choice" programs in the mid-80's. These programs have the common goal of employing competitive "market" pressures to motivate schools to improve their performance. The first "choice" program adopted by the Legislature is Post Secondary Enrollment Options, which allows eleventh and twelfth graders to take courses at state higher education institutions. The second "choice" program successfully advocated by the Partnership provides that any student in any Minnesota school district (with a few exceptions) can choose to attend school in any other public school district in the state. The state aid dollars associated with that student will travel to the student's new school district. (p. 14)

Even in 1988, Lionel Barber wrote about the genesis of choice in the *Financial Times* of London: "The initial push for change came from state businesses. Some 40 Fortune 500 companies have headquarters in Minnesota and many in the 1970's were becoming alarmed at the decline in quality of school recruits" (Randall and Geiger 1991: 153).

A survey of the work and publications of the Minnesota Business Partnership suggests that decline in the quality of school recruits was less a concern than was government spending and taxes. In a list of thirty-four *Research Reports* sponsored by the partnership from 1984 to 1990, three (including the Berman and Weiler report) deal with education and at least twenty focus on government spending, taxes, and/or the cost of doing business in Minnesota. In a 1990 report, "Solving the State's Fiscal Crisis," the partnership recommended that the legislature solve the budget shortfall "through state spending reductions as opposed to tax increases." In a preview of fiscal years 1992–93, the partnership projects that spending growth will continue to exceed tax revenues and states, "This growth must be slowed" (*Resource Book* 1990–1991: 12).

The business of business is profit. Taxes cut into profits and can slow economic development. Education is expensive and takes a major share of the tax dollar. While Minnesota ranks at the top in terms of education performance, it also ranks relatively high on the Wall Chart (eighteen out of fifty) for expenditures per pupil. That means that thirty-two states spend less per pupil. The good news is that Minnesotans get what they pay for. The bad news is there's no such thing as a free lunch. Minnesota, as well as most other states, is in a period of real budget crisis. To make matters worse, add the perception of education crisis and you get the ultimate fiscal nightmare. Education reform and improvement has traditionally meant more tax dollars—until choice.

Choice provides the perfect marriage of convenience for business and politics. Now you can have reform at no additional cost. Hype the "crisis," give choice top billing as reform and restructuring and a powerful coalition of business executives and politicians become the education experts of the 1990s. In California, a businessman is pushing a petition drive to put choice on the November 1992 ballot. His organization, EXCEL (Excellence through

Choice in Education), is promoting a choice plan that would allow state funds for public, private, and parochial choice. Mr. Alibrandi is counting on President Bush's support for choice to help pass the initiative. It comes as no surprise that Governor Pete Wilson and the California Business Roundtable support public school choice (Olson 1991b: 19).

"The State of California could save $10 billion if it enacted a private-school voucher plan that gave students an education 'credit card,' according to a report by the Howard Jarvis Taxpayers Foundation. Alvin Rabushka, a Hoover Institute economist who wrote the report, said such a move could cut personal income taxes in half" (*Education Week*, June 3, 1992: 2). Is choice about better education or reduced taxes?

In Indiana, another corporate alliance, Commit Inc., works to leverage educational reform from outside the system, combatively pushing the legislature to adopt parental choice (Weisman 1991: 1). In Pennsylvania, a powerful coalition lobby, including business people known as REACH (Road to Educational Achievement through Choice), has generated thousands of letters to legislators, resulting in the state Senate passing a choice plan that would allow parents to use state stipends to send their children to any public, private, or religious school (Viadero 1991: 17). As expected, this coalition included the state's powerful Catholic Conference, which enrolls over 200,000 students in its schools. What is unexpected and unique about this and other instances of the current choice advocacy is the role of the private sector.

The rhetoric is cloaked in the American flag and appeals to all. The real agendas of reducing taxes and increasing corporate profits are not included in the discussions on education and choice. They're not hidden or secret; they're as American as apple pie, too. But corporate taxes and profits don't have the "feel good" potential for sloganeering like "freedom of choice" and "competition for excellence." The fundamental question of how the profit motive will affect the educational opportunities of all students is obscured.

With the partnership of the governor and business in 1982, the bandwagon of choice was ready to roll in Minnesota. The major obstacle was the "professionals." In 1983, Governor Perpich demanded and received legislative authority for the direct appointment of the commissioner of education. This was a significant change. What had been strictly a professional State Department of Education became much more politicized. Now the governor had his PR team in place. Assistant commissioners, department heads, and officials on down the line either got on board or got off.

As Mary Jane Smetanka reported in the Minneapolis *Star Tribune*,

> Many in the Department of Education disliked their new role of being more responsive to the governor, a position that some thought compromised the department's mission. Instead of being experts when they testified at the Legislature, they became people pushing Perpich's agenda. "It's really not Ruth Randall's [appointed commissioner by Perpich in 1983] fault, it's a political situation," said a veteran administrator who asked to remain unnamed. "We're really trying to promote the governor now, and not promoting the kids and education. The department also experienced considerable upheaval during Randall's tenure, with many veteran employees departing and much turnover among high-level administrators in the system. (Smetanka 1989: 4B)

Many see this kind of turnover and upheaval in the state education agencies as a prerequisite for change, a necessary victory over the forces of deadening bureaucracy and a lethargic education establishment bent on protecting the status quo. Osborne and Gaebler call it "bureaucratic gridlock" (Olson 1992b: 1). Blaming the bureaucracy is an integral part of the rhetoric on the crisis in education. A 1991 report by a Wisconsin think tank has recommended overhauling the state department of public instruction and making the job of its chief administrator an appointed, rather than an elected, position. The report contends that "the current structure of the agency has led to ineffectiveness in solving the state's educational problems and embracing education-reform ideas" (Wisconsin Policy Research Institute 1991: 2).

The Wisconsin report was strongly criticized by Superintendent of Public Instruction Herbert Grover. He suggested it was a "political statement" funded by business interests that support Governor Tommy G. Thompson. "While conceding that many of the institute's supporters are friends of the Governor, James Miller, the organization's executive director, said the group is nonpartisan" (p. 2). Is it coincidence that Superintendent Grover and Governor Thompson differ on the issues of choice and vouchers? (Shapiro 1991: 57–58). Is this a battle of bureaucracy at the state level or a power struggle over deregulation of education and the subsequent reduction of education expenditures?

Pipho reports that in Florida as well, part of Governor Chiles's plan to bail education out of a budget shortfall was a proposal to deregulate the schools and suggests that other governors are "even using the economic downturn as the impetus to restructure the ways their states deliver and serve education" (Pipho 1991a: 656). Is this all about bureaucracy or balancing budgets?

In Minnesota, regulation is out and choice is in. The first legislation of choice in Minnesota came through last-minute political maneuvering in a special session of the State Legislature held from June 19 to June 21, 1985. It was the Post-Secondary Enrollment Options (PSEO) program. Minnesota statute states that the purpose of the PSEO program is "to promote rigorous academic pursuits and to provide a wider variety of options to high school pupils" (MS. 123.3514, Sec. 1, Subd. 2). The program enables eleventh- and twelfth-grade public school students to enroll in Minnesota post-secondary institutions on a full- or part-time basis and to receive dual credit, both secondary and post-secondary. As Jessie Montano explains: "An appropriation for the cost of students' tuition, fees and textbooks was not included; rather, these expenses are paid by the state 'foundation aid' which students generate for their districts. Thus, dollars follow students" (Nathan 1989: 168).

Participation in the PSEO program has grown from 3,500 students during the first year, 1985–86, to 6,600 during the 1990–91 school year. During 1990–91, approximately 2,500 students enrolled full or part time in the community colleges, 1,800 at the University of Minnesota, 1,300 at area technical colleges, 600 in the state university system, and 350 in the private college system. Since there are no ongoing monitoring or evaluation programs in place, this kind of information is available only through interviews with state department personnel. How many of the 6,600 enrolled in 1990–91 were successful? No one at the state level knows or is asking that kind of question.

Example. Jane would have graduated from high school in June 1991. She had excellent attendance throughout her high school career and maintained a grade point average of 2.608 at the end of her junior year. However, in the fall of her senior year, she enrolled full time at a community college. Jane says her father really pushed her to go. He wanted her to get one free year of college and she agreed, looking forward to a more mature social life. However, Jane failed or received incomplete grades in all of her courses for the first two quarters and never attended at all after enrolling in the spring quarter. She did not graduate and she did not receive any college credit. She moved out of her home during this process and in the winter of 1992 was doing nothing about her education, was very depressed and calling herself a failure.

How many Janes are there? How many students are using PSEO simply to get one or two free years of college at the same time that they are earning their diploma? According to former Commissioner Randall, the only PSEO evaluation in Minnesota is "a local foundation [that] is funding a university fellow who is conducting a study which will provide information on the number of dropouts who have returned to school, level of satisfaction, change in expectations and aspirations, and the like" (Randall and Geiger 1991: 125). The study was completed in December 1990 by Joe Nathan and Wayne Jennings with the support of the Joyce Foundation. The study includes four choice programs in Minnesota. However, three of the four programs are categorical in the sense that they are targeted at specific or qualifying populations of students. The inclusion of PSEO, an across-the-board program for any student, any district, or any institution, in a study with the other specific programs tends to obscure what the study doesn't tell us. This study wasn't looking for Jane.

The study begins with the personal stories of five students for whom choice was successful: "This report describes the experiences of young people such as those described above: the more than 13,000 Minnesota students who used several laws to take courses outside of the public secondary school in their district in the 1989–90 school year" (Nathan and Jennings 1990: 2). Although the stories are inspiring, the rhetoric surrounding them suggests that they represent the 13,000 participants. No Janes in those stories; neither is the study likely to find the Janes. The study relied exclusively on student surveys. A 10 percent computer-generated random sample was created of the 5,900 students whose districts reported that they participated in PSEO during the 1989–90 school year. Of the 590 surveys sent out, only 400 were returned, for a return rate of 67 percent (p. 30).

Were there any Janes in the 33 percent that didn't return the survey or in the 5,310 students who were not part of the stratified sample? No one knows, and no one's asking. Certainly not Mr. Nathan. He is a longtime proponent of choice and vouchers in education. His books include *Free to Teach*, in which he states: "A voucher system builds on our finest individual and collective instinct" (Nathan 1983: 147). In *Public Schools by Choice*, he concludes:

> Everyone agrees that our public schools must be improved. The percentage of students who leave prior to graduation is much too high; the percentage of students who have mastered basic and applied skills is much too low. We believe that providing choice among public schools is central to solving these problems. (Nathan 1989: 260)

This study was not designed to find negatives. The PSEO survey sent out included a checklist of fourteen reasons for choosing. Not one provided for the possibility that free college combined with a high school diploma might be a motive (Nathan and Jennings 1990: Appendix). When negatives did surface in the survey results, they are certainly not emphasized. In the section "Several findings stand out," number eight reads, "The vast majority of students reported greater success in school." However, PSEO numbers in the same section indicate that 64.5 percent did not report greater success. Mr. Nathan is a strong and sincere advocate for choice. What's necessary for evaluation of policy changes of this magnitude, however, is hard evidence and thorough and objective analysis.

Neither the Minnesota Legislature, which passed the PSEO program, nor the State Department of Education charged with implementing the program provided for any ongoing evaluation of PSEO, other than the tracking of numbers for the transfer of dollars. However, officials in the Minnesota Community College system began a study of the PSEO program in 1990. An early draft of this study raises several concerns about the program. The report makes reference to the fact that 90 percent of all young people in Minnesota graduate from high school and 90 percent of these graduates go on to some form of post-secondary education within a few years. This means that a majority of all freshmen are average or below average in academic potential (Bergstrom 1990: 9).

If the PSEO program is being used for "rigorous academic pursuits" as intended, PSEO students should receive better than average grades. However, grade data collected by the State Department of Education on 1985–86 PSEO students and reported in 1987 indicate that the 49 percent of PSEO students attending community colleges had lower grades than other PSEO students. One explanation suggested was that more PSEO students in community colleges were average or below average in high school achievement than was the case for most other PSEO institutions (Bergstrom 1990: 9).

A survey of admission requirements in all eighteen community colleges and representative institutions in other post-secondary systems suggest another explanation. Most other systems have higher admissions requirements than community colleges. Of the eighteen community colleges, ten reported "open door," no criteria, counseling, or guidelines (Bergstrom 1990: 26):

> A report from Legislative Research indicates that several state universities admit approximately one-third of new students from the lower half in high school rank. Two-year colleges probably admit more than one-third from the lower half of high school class rank. (p. 9)

While these admissions practices may be consistent with the original missions of these institutions, they are not necessarily consistent with a program for high school students that seeks to promote rigorous academic pursuit.

The community college study revealed a far more alarming concern than the lower grades of PSEO students. They began to find the Janes. A grade distribution report of the Community College System for 1989–90 PSEO students found that of those students taking two or more courses per term, almost half did not complete one or more courses during the year. However, the data collected are confusing. "Drops" are the largest single factor in non-completions and may reflect some students who registered in the spring but decided over the summer to remain in high school (an administrative as well as data analysis nightmare). The study discounted most "drops" and estimated that one-third of the students taking two or more courses in any one term had at least one unsatisfactory result (p. 18).

Simply stated, the concern is that PSEO students of average academic ability are being admitted as full-time college students and too often drop out of college. The problem is that these students have also become high school drop-outs. On a more positive note, North Hennepin Community College instituted higher admissions standards for PSEO students in 1989–90 and had a 40 percent reduction in the proportion of PSEO students who did not complete courses successfully (p. 30). The frustration is that these concerns were raised in 1984–85, but no one listened. As early into the PSEO program as the 1986–87 school year, counselors from Governor Perpich's own Hibbing High School were raising concerns about the consequence of no admission standards.

Finally, and through no effort on the part of the Legislature or the State Department of Education, the Community College System has adopted minimum admission standards for PSEO students statewide. However, they will not be fully in effect until the 1992–93 school year. From 1985 to 1992, a lot of Janes paid for a hastily enacted, poorly implemented political compromise. The new standards (a 3.0 grade point average or top 25 percent for juniors and 2.5 grade point average or top 50 percent for seniors) would still have allowed Janes to participate and are probably not high enough to "promote rigorous academic pursuits," but are at least the first steps in addressing a major blunder. Further steps, however, seem doubtful unless much more study and evaluation is completed. Bergstrom called for at least seven or eight types of additional information and evaluation to be completed, including follow-up studies of PSEO students. All of these suggestions for further study focus on the post-secondary perspective. None focuses on what's happening back in the local school district as a result of PSEO.

Officials at the Minnesota State Department of Education report that in 1989–90, approximately $4.2 million was transferred from local school districts to post-secondary institutions due to PSEO participation. During the 1991 legislative session, amendments were added to the PSEO program, providing a new method of transferring aid between school districts and post-secondary institutions. This new method is another reduction in aid to local school districts and, according to state department personnel, will result in an additional $4.5 million being lost to local school districts for approximately the same number of PSEO enrollments in 1991–92. What effect does this loss of revenue have on local schools?

Example. Joe was an all-around good student. He had letters in three sports during his sophomore and junior years, was elected a class officer for his senior year and graduated in the top 10 percent of his class of seventy-five seniors. In the spring of his junior year, he was looking forward to a great senior year before going to college to major in engineering. However, his registration for senior courses included calculus and physics. Both were cut because five of his classmates opted to go to a community college full time and the school district could not afford to offer the classes for only two or three students. Joe's parents and older sister had attended and graduated from the local high school and he wanted to participate in the same tradition. But others' "choices" had eliminated his "choice." In order to continue his college prep schedule of courses, Joe was forced to go to college. Joe's parents could not afford a third car. Although Joe completed the college courses and graduated with his class in June 1991, the logistics of transportation prevented him from maintaining his high school athletic and extra-curricular participation. He says that part of his youth was stolen from him.

How many Joes are there? What are the effects of PSEO on the local school districts? Is there a "brain drain"? What cuts are made as the students and aids flow to the post-secondary schools?

Example. Mr. Johnson is a frustrated father. He has to drive his children past his local elementary school so they can attend first, fourth, and fifth grade in the neighboring community where he works. He and his wife used open enrollment for their three children to escape large class sizes and combination grades. He attended a local school board meeting to question elementary staffing policies and the fact that while elementary class size was increasing, new classes with very small enrollments were being added at the high school. He was told that the high school courses were added to keep more students from going to college and that the additional costs had to be balanced by elementary cuts. One board member stated that the elementary cuts were relatively invisible in the new competitive world of education.

Confusing, isn't it? Joe's school district cuts high school classes because of PSEO and Mr. Johnson's adds high school classes—but at the expense of elementary class size and combination grades. The problem is that no consideration or direction was given to local school districts as they coped with the losses of students and state aids to PSEO. Virtually no state attention has been focused on this issue, to identify, study, or evaluate the effects of PSEO on local school districts.

Interviews with school district and college personnel around the state revealed several other concerns. Many counselors, in both high school and college, indicated that access to a job market was a major consideration for many PSEO students. In addition, students could escape the long, seven-hour days of high school and arrange their schedules around their jobs. One student explained very candidly that you have to be really stupid not to figure it out. You have to spend 170 class periods at high school to get a credit and you can get the same credit at college for only 120 class periods.

Counselors also reported that many students were using PSEO as an excuse to "get away from home" and parental restrictions a year or two early. One principal said that in discussion, he and his colleagues had detected a pattern in some of their PSEO enrollments. He indicated that many mature girls who had socialized with and dated older students throughout junior and senior high school were going to college because their social life was "boring" by eleventh and twelfth grade.

One community college counselor, on the receiving end of the PSEO students, remarked that the program was demoralizing to both the college and high school teachers. College staff members felt that the PSEO students, many just sixteen years old, were not prepared to do college work. They felt they were faced with the difficult decision of failing or "washing-out" many of these students or reducing their academic standards to the high school level. There's little doubt how this dilemma will be solved if and when the college administration becomes worried about declining numbers and fewer dollars.

When average or below average students go from high school classes to the colleges, high school teachers question the worth of their work. If the last two years of high school are not required of even average students who are free to go, why are they required at all? It does seem ironic that Minnesota passed the PSEO, which lessens the amount of formal schooling required of PSEO students by two years, yet it also passed legislation in the 1991 session that will add twenty days of instruction to the public school calendar beginning in 1995–96. One wonders if there is any comprehensive planning or sense of direction behind Minnesota's educational policies.

High school counselors expressed frustration because there was little timely communication with the colleges about students' grades, particularly failures and incompletes. Students like Jane get lost in the "which counselors are to blame" shuffle. Who's responsible for these students? Should college counselors be expected to call parents when students are in academic or attendance trouble? When students fail a class at college, they fail to graduate at high school. Deadlines at the high school for credit counts, certification for graduation, printing of diplomas, ordering of announcements, caps and gowns, and so on do not mesh neatly with the college grade reporting schedules. Horror stories abound of PSEO students either included in the high school yearbooks when they shouldn't have been or excluded when they should have been included.

In several school districts, principals reported students leaving high school to avoid tough courses or instructors. Courses at the community colleges for the same credit were easier to "ace." Those high school instructors were feeling increasing pressure to reduce the expectations, the amount of reading or writing, in order to stem the flow. Confusing again. In some cases, PSEO students can't meet the higher academic standards at college, and in other cases, they leave high school to escape high academic standards.

Free college, access to jobs, easier schedules, the dating game— there was absolutely no attempt in structuring PSEO legislation to ensure that the motives for PSEO participation matched the intent of the law. If the intention was to provide a wider variety of options, then the program would have provided college enrollment and state aid only for courses not available at the high school. If the intention was to promote rigorous academic pursuits, then the program would have required higher admission standards for PSEO students than were required of incoming freshmen.

What was the intention? The test of good laws and program implementation is that they accomplish only what they set out to do and no more. A good law and implementation also provides ongoing monitoring and evaluation to ensure a match between intent and consequence. Minnesota's Post-Secondary Enrollment Options fails on all counts.

3

Choice and Open Enrollment

Open enrollment, the second and most momentous of Minnesota's choice programs successfully advocated by the Minnesota Business Partnership, was first passed by the 1987 Legislature and was effective for the 1987–88 school year. School districts were not required to participate in the open enrollment program (the Enrollment Options Program) during the first two years, 1987–88 and 1988–89. The 1988 Legislature mandated open enrollment beginning with the 1989–90 school year for districts with more than a thousand students in grades K–12, and for all districts beginning with the 1990–91 school year.

The program allows students in grades K–12 to enroll in school districts other than the one in which the student lives. All school districts must let their students go, but all districts do not have to accept open enrollment students. A school district may declare itself closed by school board resolution. The only school district to declare itself closed was the wealthy, predominantly white suburb of Edina, Minnesota. Under heavy criticism for elitism, Edina reversed its decision in the second year. The only limitations in this otherwise unrestricted, laissez-faire choice program involve three districts (Duluth, Minneapolis, and St. Paul), which operate under desegregation guidelines. These districts may limit the students transferring in and out to ensure that the districts remain in compliance with their desegregation plan. The full state aids for each student (including general education revenue, capital expenditure equipment and facilities revenue, and transportation revenue) are transferred from the student's resident district to the district of choice (Urahn 1990: 5).

There are many questions and concerns regarding the implementation of the open enrollment program. Most of these will be addressed specifically in succeeding chapters on the topics of governance, finance, winners/losers, and equity. However, it is useful at this point to examine whether the open enrollment program meets the tests of a good law. A major component of the test requires an evaluation and assessment to ensure that the law does what it was intended to do. Minnesota has attempted to evaluate the results of open enrollment in three working papers published by the Research Department of the House of Representatives.

Harsh criticism has been leveled against Minnesota for prematurely praising its open enrollment program. Former Governor Perpich and Commissioner Randall traveled the country promoting similar choice programs before the program was fully implemented and before the first assessment was completed. The *Arizona Republic* was already calling Governor Perpich the "Pied Piper of Choice" in early 1989. No assessments or evaluations have been conducted since the program was fully implemented in 1990–91. The three working papers were all completed using 1989–90 data, a full year before the smallest school districts in Minnesota were mandated to participate. Yet the first working paper begins: "Education secretary Lauro Cavazos said, 'Where choice is used, it works. . . . Choice allows schools to draw strength from diversity by developing different programs. It allows each school to excel' " (Urahn 1990: 1).

"It works," opens the first assessment, although both the second and third working papers include disclaimers about not being comprehensive evaluations. "Since the program's first full year of implementation is 1990–91, it would be premature to attempt to evaluate it at this stage" (Urahn 1991a: 2; 1991b: 3).

This kind of contradictory rhetoric and generalization is evident throughout the working papers. The most significant contradiction throughout the papers revolves around the reasons students and parents gave for choosing open enrollment. It also identifies a fundamental flaw in the rationale for choice. During the 1989–90 school year, students and parents applying for open enrollment were not required to state their reasons for transfer. The 1990 Legislature amended the program to require that reasons be stated on the applications for open enrollment beginning with the 1990–91 school year. In 1989–90, only 34 percent of the participants volunteered reasons (Urahn 1991b: 5). Of the reasons given, over 40 percent were "convenience" and 6 percent included extra-curricular, athletic, or social explanations (Urahn, 1990: 20). Thus, close to 50 percent of the reasons given have absolutely nothing to do with access to excellence. One can only guess about the motives of the 66 percent who would not volunteer their reasons. It seems reasonable to surmise that the motives people refused to reveal had even less to do with excellence and academics.

The three working papers represent the total of Minnesota's assessment of open enrollment. The first paper, "Student and District Participation 1989–90," was completed in February 1990 and was intended to be a descriptive analysis, including reasons for participation. The most valuable data included in this paper are found in its Appendix B, "Student Transfer Under Open Enrollment by District: 1989–90" (Urahn 1990: 24–31). This is an eight-page chart of all Minnesota school districts, with columns for total district enrollment, total number of students leaving, total number of students entering, net gain (+ or –), and percent of enrollment change by school district. With this chart, one can easily identify winners and losers in the first year of mandatory participation for districts with a thousand or more students.

One of the main concerns about open enrollment has been that a district suffering a net loss of students and revenue in the first round of choice would enter a downward spiral. The revenue losses would force cuts in program that would prompt more students to leave, causing further cuts, and so on. An examination of the chart of transfers by district for the second and succeeding years would be the logical next step in testing the hypothesis. However, officials at the House Research Department and the State Department of Education indicate that similar data are no longer being compiled, not even for 1990–91, the first year of full mandatory participation and the year in which the smallest, most vulnerable districts participated. Any reasonable assessment to determine the consequences of the legislation would seem to require this kind of data analysis for several years. Is it money, staff time, or lack of interest in the outcomes?

Example. Losing School District 1 had a total K–12 enrollment of 1,350 students going into the 1989–90 school year. The district lost 45 students to open enrollment in 1989–90 and approximately $200,000 in revenue as a result. The district had no surplus fund balance to absorb the loss. In the early spring of 1990, the administration and school board began proposing reductions in the budget for 1990–91. With some administrative, custodial, and nursing service cuts, only 4.5 full-time equivalent (FTE) classroom teachers were proposed for lay-offs. However, this would result in larger class sizes at two elementary grade levels and the loss of one foreign language and five other elective courses in the high school curriculum. Many parents attending the budget meeting in February 1990 were members of the Band Boosters and were particularly upset over proposed reductions in the instrumental music program that would eliminate the summer band program and reduce lesson time at the junior and senior high level. As a result of these reductions, thirty-two students applied to open enrollment transfer for the 1990–91 school year. The district had to prepare for another round of cuts to absorb the additional loss of $140,000 for the next school year. Board members expressed frustration and indicated that they felt trapped in a no-win dilemma. How could they keep or add programs to hold or attract students when they had to cut programs to comply with the budget requirements?

How many districts are in a similar situation? Without an ongoing program of assessment and evaluation, the question will go unanswered. What programs are being cut in the losing districts? How do "frills" compare from one district to another? What if music programs or nursing services are being cut across the state? Is this kind of information relevant? Should we care about the kinds of reductions being made in response to open enrollment?

The only attempt to get this kind of information came in the second working paper, "Survey of School District Superintendents, 1989–90." All 433 superintendents were sent surveys, but only 316 were included in the analysis. The other 28 percent either didn't respond or supervised districts that didn't participate in open enrollment during the 1989–90 school year. Again, we're missing critical information from the smallest school districts. When asked what changes occurred in districts because of open enrollment, the report states in bold type, "A change in class size was the effect most often reported." In small type later in the section, we learn "An increase was the most common type of change in class size reported" (Urahn, 1991a: 5). One has to read carefully to get past the emphasis to the whole story. In addition, the questions were general, so the answers were general and without any specifics. We still don't know, for example, if music is being cut across the state.

This biased analysis is found again in a discussion of superintendents' responses to the effects of open enrollment on cooperation among school districts. The analysis opens by stating that 20 percent of the districts indicated that open enrollment did affect interdistrict cooperation and that the most common effect was initiation or consideration of some type of cooperation. Later in the same section we learn that a number of school districts reported that open enrollment "poisoned the atmosphere" of cooperation between districts, and a small number reported that existing cooperation agreements were threatened by the loss of open enrollment students (Urahn 1991a: 7–8). On the one hand we get 20 percent of districts initiating cooperation, on the other hand we get unspecified numbers of districts.

Superintendents also reported other effects that are of some concern. One of the "benefits" reported was the loss of "marginal" and "unhappy" students and the gain of good, highly motivated students (Urahn 1991a: 3). When some students are seen as more desirable than others, what effect does that have on the school districts' public relations efforts to attract students to their district? Will brochures and radio ads emphasize information for all or only desirable students? Will programs for students with emotional and behavior disorders (EBD) be described in as much detail as winning athletic records or advanced academic offerings?

The third working paper, "Patterns of Student Transfer 1989–90," was completed in March 1991. Its intent was to explore "whether students consistently transferred to districts that differed from their resident district with respect to such district characteristics as financial resources, size, staffing patterns, interdistrict cooperation, spending and curriculum" (Urahn 1991b: 3). This study is the most sophisticated of the three, including several footnoted references to statistical significance, T-tests, standard deviations, and over fifty charts and graphs in only fifty-three pages. All of this analytical effort is applied to not one additional source of information or data for the 1989–90 school year. All of this analysis is based on the same surveys and enrollment data as for the 1989–90 school year. It should be noted that while that data were used to determine that 3,218 students participated in open enrollment during the 1989–90 school year, "the final official count conducted by the department of education will not be finalized until early in 1991. That count will undoubtedly differ from this count, both in total and at the district level" (p. 53).

Simply stated, this report superimposed the 1989–90 enrollment data on other sets of data—often from other sources and other school years—in order to discover (create) patterns. That's not too difficult when the conclusions are already drawn. Existing data are manipulated and massaged until the desired patterns emerge. When troublesome data won't cooperate, they are simply left out. As the report explains:

> The 346 students who transferred from Mt. Iron-Buhl to Virginia and from Anoka to Brooklyn Center in 1989–90 are not included in this analysis. Because many of the students in

those districts transferred for reasons unique to the districts involved, including them would bias the search for patterns based on a broad range of district characteristics. (p. 3)

Lewis Finch is more complete and accurate in his description of the students who left the Mt. Iron-Buhl school district.

Owing to a split in the community over the school board's decision to close one of the two senior high schools, a group of parents enrolled their children in a neighboring school system. The parents' move was not intended to improve the quality of the children's education; it was an act of defiance and retaliation, in which children were made pawns in a political chess game. This case, I believe, foreshadows the future. (Finch 1989: 14–15)

These districts are not anomalous in any way. They are very real examples of what can happen in unrestricted school choice. They represent the first "black eyes" of open enrollment. They are the worst-case scenarios made possible by the laissez-faire open enrollment program. Such things weren't supposed to happen; they are a major embarrassment for the choice promoters, and so they are left out of the evaluation. The report refers to similar instances that have surfaced in two more communities during the 1990–91 school year. These cases, however, will not be left out of future data analysis because no further evaluation is planned by either the House Research Department or the State Department of Education as of this writing.

In late November 1991, an official at the State Department indicated that more current data, specifically the numbers and the reasons for transfer (which are now required on the open enrollment applications) from the 1990–91 school year were being included in a federal report due in 1992. The official indicated that any future analysis was out of his hands. Given the Bush administration's push for choice as a national imperative, I don't expect to find Janes or Joes or state-wide music cuts included in that report either.

The third working paper opens with the conclusion that "most open enrollment students chose districts as 'healthy' or 'healthier' than their own district" (Urahn 1991b: 1). Unhealthy districts were described as those that were very small, poor, shared grades with another district, were losing enrollment, or had teachers with less training and experience. A follow-up conclusion was that "most students chose to attend districts with relatively high levels of teacher training and experience" (p. 30). A detailed and complex explanation of the Training and Experience (T&E) index is explained in text and footnote. Yet not one of the reasons given by parents or students relates even remotely to the T&E index. This is clearly a case of overinterpreting unrelated data to create a nonexistent correlation between two disparate variables. Is this coincidence, correlation, causation, or anything necessary to support the policy? It gets even worse.

The most blatant example occurs when searching for a pattern of student participation related to curriculum. The 1989–90 open enrollment numbers were superimposed on curriculum rating data by school district from the 1987–88 school year reported in December 1988, by the legislative auditor (Urahn 1991b: 44). The paper concludes that in the metropolitan area, 1989–90 students from districts with lower rated 1987–88 curricula were more likely to participate in open enrollment. In greater Minnesota, 1989–90 open enrollment students came disproportionately from districts with lower 1987–88 academic ratings. This creates the impression that choices were made for academic reasons.

The first problem with this, of course, is that less than 20 percent of the reasons given for transfer had anything to do with academics. More importantly, the academic ratings assigned to school districts were based exclusively on secondary curriculum measures, such as high school accreditation, honors classes, advanced placement classes, the number of foreign languages provided on site, or the number of science courses provided on site. While the curriculum was rated by secondary criteria, the table used to illustrate this analysis, "Participation in Open Enrollment by Summary Curric- ulum Measures," includes the more than 1500 elementary students that participated in 1989–90 (Urahn 1991b: 36). Combining sec- ondary curriculum factors with the elementary transfer numbers and implying that any relationship exists between the two is illogical at best, pure propaganda at worst. In addition, as the earlier analysis of the same data reports, of the reasons given by students and parents, "convenience reasons apply primarily to elementary level students" (Urahn 1990: 20). These working pa- pers were produced in a pro-choice environment to meet obligatory assessment responsibilities and were not designed to find out what is actually going on out in the trenches as a consequence of choice.

Some pieces of information are totally absent from the reports. All indications are that transportation is out of control as a result of choice. The only mention of transportation in the three papers is in the first: "The nonresident district must provide transportation within that district if the parent of a nonresident student requests it. However, the student must get to the border of the nonresident district' (Urahn 1990: 5). However, the 1990 Legislature amended the program to provide that a parent may submit a written request to the resident district asking that it allow the nonresident district to provide transportation for the pupil within the pupil's resident district. The resident district must approve or disapprove the request in writing within 30 days. The parent or guardian may appeal the refusal of the resident district to the commissioner of education. The commissioner must act on the appeal within 30 days.

An invasion of sorts marked the opening of school in northern Minnesota last week when the Northome-Indus school dis- trict sent school buses rumbling across enemy lines. It's a scene that will be repeated throughout the state this year, thanks to the latest twist in Minnesota's open-enrollment law. (Hotakainen 1990: 1B)

According to State Department officials, by November 1991, 831 appeals (representing 453 families) had been granted by the commissioner, and few had been denied. One superintendent reported three buses from different districts meeting on one intersection in his district. Another superintendent reported his district being "raided" by buses from four different districts.

In response to a board query about seeing buses from other districts coming into its district, especially when enrollments were going down, the superintendent responded, "This is the most inefficient, ridiculous ruling that has come out on open enrollment" (Albertson 1991a: 1).

A small town weekly headlined an article "They're Taking Our Children . . . And The State Says It's OK." The article began: "It is early in the morning. The sun is just coming up. A yellow vehicle glides down the country road. It stops. A youngster hops in and it takes off. Another child is being taken from his school, his town, to go to the big school in another town" (Albertson 1991c: 11).

Athletic transfers and recruiting may be another area out of control with open enrollment. Although Virginia, Minnesota assistant hockey coach Nick Novak (also the school district's public relations director) was censured by the Minnesota State High School League in May 1992 for his role in trying to recruit students, the censure only amounts to a "verbal wrist-slap" (Mossberger 1992b: 1E). This is the first such censure since open enrollment was passed. "School districts shall not compete with one another for the enrollment of students" (Minnesota Education Laws 1991, Chapter 123.35, subd. 14: 235). Not only is general recruiting prohibited by state law, it is also against Minnesota State High School League rules to recruit students from other districts on the basis of extra-curricular offerings. However, there has been little emphasis on monitoring or enforcement.

"Psst! Hey, kid, c'mere. Listen, you're pretty good with the puck, kid, but nobody's ever going to notice you at this school. Not enough horses. No, what you need is to come on over to our school and play with the big boys. What do you say, kid? You want college recruiters and NHL scouts to see you, don't you? You know how much it costs to go to college these days? Think you can save enough mowing lawns or flippin' burgers over the summer? And how about your folks? Way things are going, your old man might not even have a job next year, let alone help put you through college. Just think how proud they'd be if you helped our school into the state tournament and then got a free ride to college. Think about it, kid. But remember: This is between you and me. OK? You never saw me. If anybody asks, tell them you switched because your old high school didn't offer French" (Mossberger 1992a: 1B).

That account is fictional, but according to Skip Peltier, associate director of the state high school league, the concern is that recruiting is "being done behind closed doors, where no one can prove it. It's a very difficult rule to uphold: we have to rely on the integrity of schools and their people to not recruit for athletics" (Mossberger 1992a: 3B). According to the hockey coach in Hibbing, Minnesota, academic reasons are not accounting for most open enrollment transfers. "I think 90 percent of the kids are doing it for extra-curricular activities. I know there is a lot of this contact going on because of open enrollment. The school districts are trying to drum up kids" (Mossberger 1992a: 3B). "We're not doing anything the other schools don't do," said the Virginia superintendent (Mossberger 1992b: 1E).

In the Virginia case, recruitment letters were sent to students of other districts who happened also to be hockey players. According to the head hockey coach, "They've been advertising to draw more kids. The more kids you have, the more money the school gets. I just know I had nothing to do with any letters" (Mossberger 1992a: 3B).

Whether by coach or by district, athletic recruiting is likely to increase as a result of an amendment passed by the Minnesota State High School League's representative assembly. This amendment makes students eligible to compete in a sport at a new school if they are in attendance on opening day, and if they were eligible at their old school on the last day of the previous school year (Mossberger 1992a: 3B). Ironically, this amendment was passed in May 1992, the same month that the league issued its first recruiting censure. The right hand does not seem to know what the left hand is doing.

This is illustrative of the entire set of confusing and contradictory messages open enrollment sends to school districts. Open enrollment mandates that districts "shall make information about the district, schools, programs, policies, and procedures available to all interested people" (Minnesota Education Laws 1991, Chapter 120.06, subd. 11: 42). Yet other laws and rules prohibit competing for enrollment and recruiting for athletics. Where is the line between information and recruitment? Unsolicited personal letters to selected students fall on what side of the line? It would seem that the closer a district gets to the line, the more effective the informational program, the more students transfer and the more dollars that flow in. Which agency is responsible for monitoring the line—the high school league that regulates athletics or the legislature than opened the door? Are young athletes being hurt while the responsibility shuffle takes place at the agency level? What about the athlete who transfers on the first day of school but doesn't make the team in November? What about the transfer athlete who does make the team, at the expense of a local player? What about the players on the home team who lost their star? What about friendships and loyalties and community spirit? Do we really want this kid of activity at the high school level?

Other areas of athletic eligibility can also slip through the cracks in the open enrollment system. Students who lose academic eligibility due to low grades, suffer an alcohol, drug, tobacco, or disciplinary suspension, or fail to receive medical clearance, can simply transfer to a new district. The transferring paperwork is frequently tied up or lost between different departments of different districts. Tracking procedures depend on the diligence and integrity of many people and are inconsistent at best. Just how bad is it or could it become? No one knows and, so far, no one is asking. No new monitoring procedures or staff people have been put in place at the state level. Unfortunately, it will probably require some major tragedy or scandal before the impacts of open enrollment on high school athletics receive the necessary scrutiny and assessment.

Other information not provided in any of the state open enrollment assessments is even more disturbing. The 3,218 students participating in the 1989–90 school year represented an increase of over 800 percent from the previous year's participation of 343 students. Officials at the House Research Department indicate that unofficial open enrollment numbers for 1990–91 represent 6,100 participants in open enrollment, an 89 percent increase. In December 1991, Peggy Hunter, enrollment options coordinator for the Minnesota Department of Education, reported to the *Hibbing Daily Tribune*, "Statewide, 13,940 students took advantage of open enrollment in the 1991–92 school year" (Bloomquist 1991: 12). That represents a 128 percent increase from the previous year. Short-sighted proponents of choice have frequently chided critics for predicting a mass exodus of students with open enrollment that never materialized. I don't recall using the term, but it's clear the mass exodus doesn't occur all at once (except in some cases), but is an accelerating increase in the number of students leaving their resident districts.

However, the percentages tell only part of the story. The 3,218 students who transferred under open enrollment in 1989–90 represent approximately $16 million transferred from losing school districts. When PSEO is included, the figure for 1989–90 is closer to $20 million. Estimates of preliminary numbers for both enrollment options programs in 1990–91 meant transfers of over $34 million from losing school districts for the next year. For the 1991–92 school year, the transfer of aid following students from their resident districts will approximate over $80 million.

Massive change and restructuring have been set in motion and no one has a clue about the outcomes. Statewide, this is not an immediate, headline-producing, mass exodus in reaction to open enrollment, but a steady, inexorable erosion of the public school system in many communities. The tragedy is that while Minnesota was the first "choice" state and is being touted by the secretary and president as a model for the nation, there's little opportunity for others to benefit from the Minnesota experience. There is no ongoing assessment being conducted, and what assessment exists is incomplete and biased.

As a skeptical Wisconsin district administrator wrote,

> Education affects children as significantly as the field of medicine and yet it would be unthinkable to expose all children in Minnesota to an experimental drug in the fashion that Governor Perpich has exposed children to the choice plan. It is very difficult to be positive when I see a sound school system thrown topsy turvy with no research available to show that open enrollment programs have raised student achievement. (Randall and Geiger 1991: 132)

The rationale for open enrollment was to give students access to excellence, but they left for convenience. The assessment to track intent and consequence tells only part of the story, leaves "bad" data out, and creates statistical patterns to reaffirm popular policy. Minnesota's open enrollment, like Post Secondary Enrollment Options, fails all tests of good law.

4

Choice and Governance

> Precisely at high noon, as Reagan became president, his newly
> appointed presidential assistant for management, John Rogers, and
> four assistants briskly moved into the Oval Office and began
> rearranging the furniture. . . . Down came the presidential portraits
> of Jefferson and Truman. Lincoln remained in place. (Johnson
> 1991: 93–94)

Perhaps this is aptly symbolic of many changes to come. Lincoln,
the rugged individual, remains, while Jefferson, the believer in the
masses and the virtue of the common man, comes down. The
American agenda shifts from an emphasis on the common good to
the "me first" decade. The new direction quickly became evident
in education as well as other fields.

The wisdom of Jefferson and the founding fathers was soon
forgotten. It is worth a brief re-examination to get our bearings in
this time of rapid change and restructuring. Jefferson clearly
believed that one of the basic needs of a democratic society was
popular education: "If a nation expects to be ignorant and free, in
a state of civilization, it expects what never was and never will be"
(Jefferson 1939: 231).

Jefferson was not alone in this understanding. James Madison argued that "a publicly supported system of education would counter the monopoly of superior information otherwise enjoyed by the rich." And it would simultaneously supply "the best security against crafty and dangerous encroachments on the public safety." He described a balance of "liberty and learning, each leaning on the other for their mutual and surest support" (Sheffer 1991: 482).

Jefferson's oft-quoted argument for a free press was linked absolutely to his support for popular education. As he wrote in 1787,

> The basis of our governments being the opinion of the people, the very first object should be to keep that right; and were it left to me to decide whether we should have a government without newspapers, or newspapers without a government, I would not hesitate a moment to prefer the latter. But I should mean that every man should receive those papers, and be capable of reading them. (Jefferson 1939: 143)

Jefferson also knew that education would result in taxes. As he wrote in 1786,

> I think by far the most important bill in our whole code, is that for the diffusion of knowledge among the people. . . . Preach, my dear Sir, a crusade against ignorance; establish and improve the law for educating the common people. Let our countrymen know, that the people alone can protect us against these evils, (misery of French from kings, nobles and priests) and that the tax which will be paid for this purpose, is not more than the thousandth part of what will be paid to kings, priests and nobles, who will rise up among us if we leave the people in ignorance. (Jefferson 1939: 134)

Public education is so inexorably tied to democracy that Jefferson believed a constitutional amendment was imperative to protect the balance.

In every government on earth is some trace of human weakness, some germ of corruption and degeneracy, which cunning will discover, and wickedness insensibly open, cultivate and improve. Every government degenerates when trusted to the rulers of the people alone. The people themselves are its only safe depositories. And to render even them safe, their minds must be improved to a certain degree. . . . An amendment of our constitution must here come in aid of the public education. The influence over government must be shared among all the people. If every individual . . . participates of the ultimate authority, the government will be safe. (Jefferson 1939: 133)

The wisdom of Madison and Jefferson was not forgotten in 1857 when the Minnesota constitution was adopted. Article XIII reads:

The stability of a republican form of government depending mainly upon the intelligence of the people, it is the duty of the legislature to establish a general and uniform system of public schools. The legislature shall make such provisions by taxation or otherwise as will secure a thorough and efficient system of public school throughout the state. (*Minnesota Legislative Manual* 1991–92: 45–46)

The understanding of Jefferson may have been remembered and echoed in 1857, but it was surely forgotten in 1988 when the legislature passed open enrollment. The Jeffersonian link between government and popular, uniform, public education is broken. With enrollment choice, it's everyone for himself. If I move my children from my local school, for whatever reason, and if my decision results in a loss of revenue for the local school, that is not my concern. I'm taking care of mine. I'm now a consumer, looking for the best deal, as admonished by the proponents of open enrollment. "Your child's needs come first," leads an article on choice in the *Minneapolis Star Tribune*, on May 6, 1991.

"Unfortunately, choosing schools is not like choosing an automobile. There's much less evaluative information about schools than there is when you choose a car, a refrigerator or a stove," cautions Joe Nathan. Have no fear, Minnesota is developing a computer system to help match families with schools and should have it operating in about a year. (Smetanka 1991: 8A)

All of this to do about choosing the right school rather misses the Jeffersonian point. As a citizen, I neither care about nor am affected by my neighbor's choice of automobile or stove or refrigerator. However, when my neighbors can choose to take their children from the local school and the state aid follows, I do care and I am affected. The resources left to educate my children in our local school are reduced. If enough leave and the school closes, my choice to enroll my children in my neighborhood school is gone. This is the ultimate myth of choice. The choices of others have diminished or eliminated my choices. In discussing the concepts of absolute freedom and the relative rights of individuals in a democracy, Justice Oliver Wendell Holmes said, "The right to swing my fist ends where the other man's nose begins."

John Kennedy put it this way, "The rights of every man are diminished when the rights of one man are threatened" (McClenaghan 1990: 16). If just one student is hurt, just one class of students neglected or just one school fails to provide equitable opportunities as a result of choice, then the experiment fails to meet its burden of proof.

Isn't the Jeffersonian point still missing? Like it or not, compatible with the "me decade" or not, I have to care about my neighbor's children's education because of my vested interest in democracy, in the stability of our republican form of government. Jefferson said that it's my protection against corruption. According to Madison, my liberty is dependent on their learning. Jefferson put it still another way:

And say, finally, whether peace is best preserved by giving

energy to the government or information to the people. This last is the most certain, and the most legitimate engine of government. Educate and inform the whole mass of the people. Enable them to see that it is their interest to preserve peace and order, and they will preserve them. (Jefferson 1939: 37)

When one examines the benefits that hang in the balance, not caring about what happens to the quality of education of others is dangerous; choice is dangerous. One has only to read Kozol's 1991 descriptions of inner city schools in *Savage Inequalities* and reflect on the Los Angeles riots following the Rodney King verdict to comprehend the danger and to appreciate the wisdom of Jefferson completely.

With open enrollment, the Minnesota constitutional terms "general," "uniform," and "thorough" fail the people of Toivola-Meadowlands and other communities in rural Minnesota as they struggle to keep their local schools open. At a school board hearing on the closing of the Toivola-Meadowlands school held in October 1991, the superintendent reported that the enrollment at the school had dropped more than 32 percent from the 1990–91 school year to the 1991–92 school year. "Open Enrollment is not very good for small schools," he stated (Albertson 1991b: 15). Community meetings of Toivola-Meadowlands residents to discuss the future of the school had turnouts of 150 to 200 people. One resident told the story of an eighty-six-year-old former Toivola-Meadowlands teacher who spoke to a community meeting. "She got up and told us we had to save our school, and when she finished she sat down and died right there in her seat. That's how important this is to people" (Helmberger 1991: 4).

The 1991–92 enrollment at the school was only 162 students in grades K–12. Perhaps this is where the other constitutional term, "efficient," applies. However, if the application is valid, the legislature would have to argue coincidence rather than intent. The rhetoric of the open enrollment proponents camouflaged or denied any consolidation agenda. The choice legislation is silent in regard to possible school closings and consolidations. The assessments of the choice programs have ignored the issue.

Efficiency is important and may even be necessary. However, if consolidation and closing of schools were agendas of the choice legislation, why the deception and dishonesty? Why not tackle the issues of costs and efficiency and consolidation courageously, head-on, where logical outcomes and consequences could be addressed? Instead, open enrollment sets in motion a Machiavellian reduction by attrition, where only the "fittest" or largest schools survive, where the smaller, community schools are defeated before the competition begins. The slow death of rural school districts and the gradual deterioration of services to a whole generation of young people will be a sad commentary on the quality of leadership in Minnesota and other choice states.

It isn't just small or rural school districts that are potential losers in the competition for numbers and dollars. Any controversy in any school district has the potential to produce the big loss entry into the downward spiral from which there may be no recovery. Prior to the 1989–90 school year, parents of more than 50 percent of the Mt. Iron-Buhl's 550 secondary students had filed for open enrollment as a result of the controversial closing of one of two high schools the previous year. The threat of this mass exodus forced the school board to reverse its decision and to reopen the Mt. Iron high school for the 1989–90 school year.

This reversal involved the second complete move of all secondary furniture, equipment and material, including the high school office, all texts and the entire library, industrial arts, home economics, and computer facilities. After all this, only half the students returned. And of course, this reversal was not well received on the Buhl end of the consolidated district, and those residents proceeded to transfer in smaller but still significant numbers. By the 1991–92 school year, the Mt. Iron-Buhl school district's enrollment had dropped from over 1,200 students in 1985–86 to 700 students, and the losses continue.

The Mt. Iron-Buhl story is only one of several in Minnesota, where controversy of one variety or another produced large out-enrollments. As reported in the state analysis, "In 1990–91, open enrollment continues to give students the opportunity to 'vote with their feet' in response to school board decisions" (Urahn 1991b: 2).

In political jargon, this is called "putting a positive spin" on disastrous situations. In 1990–91, open enrollment helped destroy a cooperative agreement between the Motley and Staples school districts and made the continuing survival of the smaller Motley district unlikely. In 1989–90, Motley had an enrollment of 494 students, but by the 1991–92 school year, over 200 students had applied to leave. The courts have already been involved, and another lawsuit was still pending an appeal in late 1991.

But the numbers tell only part of the story. These kinds of situations were not supposed to happen. They were not included in the intent of the law. Therefore, as indicated in Chapter 2, their numbers are left out of the assessments to avoid "biasing" the analysis. Advocates of choice go one step further and imply that something was fundamentally wrong in those and similar districts to begin with. "Perhaps that movement says something about the districts," says Joe Nathan (Nathan 1989: 307). This kind of unprofessional innuendo is evasive, self-serving, and simply another attempt at "positive spin." It is particularly sad because it exacerbates the problems in communities torn apart and traumatized by open enrollment.

The open enrollment fall-out in these communities is horrendous. The people from Buhl and Mt. Iron still distrust and blame each other. The animosity in Motley and Staples is even worse. District personnel in Motley indicated that people have stopped doing business with each other, have stopped speaking to one another, and in one instance, divorced one another. The irony is that this kind of chaos and hurt is focused on people, not on open enrollment. Open enrollment operates like an invisible instigator. After all, it is easier to hate each other, visible, concrete objects, than it is to hate a law or to direct anger at the abstraction of choice.

Other communities should take note. The political winds of controversy can blow into any district at any time.

Example. In Losing School District 2, an unfortunate incident in the eighth-grade coed swimming class prompted a controversy. A male student with an emotional behavior disorder touched or fondled a female student. The issue was brought before the public board meeting, and the headlines screamed. Parents turned out in large numbers at several school board meetings, demanding separate swimming classes for male and female students. When the school officials explained that they could not comply without violating federal and state requirements, the parents threatened to take their students to a neighboring district in which swimming was not part of the physical education program.

How does a school board or any governing body do its job when open enrollment allows any controversy to become a lose-lose proposition? Parents can use their children's enrollment as blackmail, and the children become hostages. Imagine the possibilities: A homosexual teacher comes out of the closet. A secretary, teacher, or student tests positive for the AIDS virus. The health instructor teaches about safe sex and the use of condoms. The teachers strike or popular teachers are laid off. It could be secular humanism versus creationism. Open enrollment leaves school boards terribly vulnerable to single-issue pressure groups.

The prospects of these kinds of student migrations raise many questions about the effects of choice on school district governance, local control, and grass roots democracy. Tough, courageous decision-making by school leaders becomes risky and increasingly unlikely. The survival of school districts, particularly smaller districts, becomes a matter of body counts and all decisions will be made with one eye on the "open" doors. In Minnesota, several communities have already paid a high price for a hastily enacted, topsy-turvy experiment.

The issue of governance is further complicated when one realizes that parents who have moved their children out of their resident district will still be voting for the school boards that no longer educate their children. They will not be able to vote for the non-resident school boards that do educate their children. When excess tax levy referenda and bond issues for capital improvement are factored in, interesting inequities surface. If your children are enrolled outside your local district, are you more or less likely to vote to increase your taxes to improve or maintain the local schools your children no longer attend? How about the other side of the coin?

Example. In Winning School District 1, the addition of over 300 open enrollment students since 1989–90 has jammed already full facilities to overflowing. The school board has to contemplate a multimillion-dollar bond issue to remodel, build, and expand facilities. Resident taxpayers are angry over the prospect of increasing their property taxes to accommodate non-resident students whose families will not be assessed any share of the tax burden because they don't own property in the district. They argue that the district shouldn't have let the students in in the first place and threaten to campaign openly to defeat the bond issue. They further threaten to file a taxpayers suit if it passes. They argue that the open enrollment parents deliberately left their resident district to avoid the costs of improving their own facilities. They can vote against taxes in their own district and let someone else pay the price for the modern facilities their children will enjoy in their new, non-resident school district.

What happens to the concept of accountability to the electorate? Isn't this a form of de facto disenfranchisement? What happens to grass-roots democracy in this "like it or leave it" choice environment?

This dismantling of local school board governance may not be all that bad, according to John Chubb and Terry Moe. In their book *Politics, Markets, and America's Schools*, they suggest that the major problem with America's schools is that they operate under direct democratic control. Presumably, this direct democratic control creates an excessive bureaucracy that destroys the autonomy of local schools by imposing "higher-order values," regulations, rules, and mandates from outside the system. Autonomy, according to the authors, explains why private schools and homogeneous suburban schools are so much better than the rest of the public schools. They conclude that "democratic control tends to promote bureaucracy, markets tend to promote autonomy" (Chubb and Moe 1990: 61).

Chubb and Moe are themselves outsiders to the educational system; both are political scientists. That makes their argument that democracy causes bureaucracy most interesting. One wonders how this explains the massive, former Soviet bureaucracy. This portion of their work is all theory, with no attempt to provide empirical evidence. Reading and re-reading this opening section of the book provoked the frequent observation: This makes no sense; they haven't been here in the schools to understand; this is not how it works. The only common-sense concept encountered was the notion that rules, regulations, and requirements are passed in response to problems, and since there are more problems in the heterogeneous, inner-city schools, there is more bureaucracy in these schools. Yet a basic inconsistency in their theory is evident when they describe bureaucrats: "The imposition of formal con-straints on those below them in the public hierarchy enhances their status, power, and opportunities" (Chubb and Moe 1990: 45). Do the regulations come as a result of problems or to meet the self-serving interests of the regulators?

Granted, problems and abuses in any human organization will bring rules or regulations to correct the situation and bureaucrats to enforce them. This is even true within the institutions of family and parenting. Curfews, grounding and withholding privileges are not necessary if the children behave like angels. What is truly amazing is that Chubb and Moe fail to understand that in their proposed open market, scholarship schools and system, the same sequence of events—problems, rules, regulators—would inevita-bly occur. They maintain that "a world of autonomous schools would be a world without educational bureaucrats" (p. 46).

Wouldn't problems or abuses that surfaced in the new choice schools generate new rules and regulations? Suppose, as some critics have suggested, that abusive "diploma mills" sprang up in the ghettos to cash in on the new availability of government tuition stipends. "Released from all but the most rudimentary certification and accreditation requirements, these schools would be free to be bad—possibly even worse than the schools they supplanted or replaced" (Lemann 1991: 104). Surely some regulation would be promulgated to prevent such problems from continuing.

In the Chubb and Moe schools, "there will be no requirements for career ladders, advisory committees, textbook selection, in-service training, homework, or anything else. The schools will be organized and operated as they see fit" (Chubb and Moe 1990: 223). Does this mean there will be no more study of irrelevant Shakespeare, or dull and boring classes in American history and government, or deadly drill and practice in mathematics, or repetitious exercises in writing and grammar? Would these schools have the usual mix of required and elective studies? If so, who would determine the required material?

What if one of these public schools is organized around neo-Nazi beliefs and teaches that the Holocaust history is exaggerated and those Jews who did perish got what they deserved? The Bill of Rights protects people's rights to hold these beliefs and even express them, but would we tolerate public tax dollars, scholarships, being used to support them? This is not an unlikely possibility. The groups exist and they would send their children. The texts are available. Wouldn't some rule or requirement be developed if this kind of abuse surfaced?

According to the authors, "even our severest critics have not raised a single question about this portion of our analysis. . . . Our critics have also had little or no quarrel with our analysis of bureaucracy" (Chubb and Moe 1991: 19). To quarrel is to defend bureaucracy, a most onerous task, as the term is frequently used as an epithet and is loaded with only negative connotations. That is precisely why the critics have left it alone. Chubb and Moe use the term perhaps more than any other in the book and get away with it because it instantly conjures up an amorphous mass of red tape, mindless bureaucrats, and countless, counter-productive constraints. It would be an entertaining exercise to trace the selective use of the term "bureaucracy." So often the bureaucracy is responsible for only those public policies one opposes, and bureaucrats administer only those programs one dislikes. Policies one supports become national imperatives, and administrators become czars and the term "bureaucracy" is conspicuously absent.

However, the term is deceptively general, and the authors avoid specifics. Definition and specifics will help evaluate their analysis. Chubb and Moe describe the educational bureaucracy as the set of form constraints, rules, and regulations imposed on public schools from above—the district, state and federal levels. In order to determine the amount and effect of bureaucracy that exists in public schools, they designed and analyzed surveys returned by 402 principals and over 10,000 teachers in 1984. The survey results were then combined with student achievement data collected in 1980 and 1982 from the same schools. "For the next several years, they crunched the numbers and probed the information looking for patterns and correlations" (Olson 1990: 48). This number crunching was quite sophisticated for two graduates of public schools.

For example, under a table of "Estimates of Final Models of Administrative and Personnel Constraint," one finds the following notes:

b. The full models also included a dummy variable for rural location and two other parent variables; parent socioeconomic status and parental relationships. The coefficients on the variables consistently proved to be nonsignificant so they were dropped from the final models reported here.

c. Coefficients are unstandardized regression coefficients; standard errors are in parentheses. Standardized regression coefficients (betas) are in italics. (Chubb and Moe 1990: 176)

Whether the standard errors are valid is for other numbers experts to cross-crunch.

John Witte, a political scientist from the University of Wisconsin at Madison, has criticized their analysis on several counts. He argues that the entire set of data used by Chubb and Moe is suspect. Witte further suggests that the authors used a number of statistical procedures that convey "a distorted picture of the learning that we might predict from reasonable changes in school organization"

(Rothman 1990: 20). J. Douglas Willms, professor of educational psychology at the University of British Columbia, agreed "that the 'weird transformation' in achievement data would result in exaggerated differences between public and private schools." He continues: "Once I got to that point, it didn't seem worth reading any further. They build in the answer they wanted to by virtue of scaling" (Rothman 1990: 20).

The problem with the numbers game is not so much which cruncher is correct, but the fact that lay readers, including most educational policymakers and media anchors, won't even read the quantitative analysis, let alone make sense out of it. This gives additional weight to any conclusions drawn from the statistical analysis. The numbers are so complicated and so precise. If the emperor ever parades naked again, the invisible cloth will, in all probability, be woven not of warp and woof but of regression coefficients and dummy variables. Let's at least question the mathematization of bureaucracy and its suggested correlation with student achievement.

Let's also break the general concept of bureaucracy into some specifics. The restrictions on corporal punishment of students are often criticized by more "old-fashioned" educators as limiting their disciplinary discretion. According to Chubb and Moe, constraints like these are imposed from above by bureaucrats to enhance their status, power and opportunities (Chubb and Moe 1990: 45). In the real world, these constraints were imposed by courts responding to problems and incidents we now call child abuse. If a child were beaten in one of the authors' market-controlled, autonomous schools, would the parents' only recourse be, as a consumer, to leave and take their "business" elsewhere? Or would outside interference impose some higher-order values to protect children?

In the proposed market-driven system, "schools must be free to expel students or deny them readmission when, based on their own experience and standards, they believe the situation warrants it (as long as they are not 'arbitrary and capricious')" (Chubb and Moe 1990: 222–23). Arbitrary and capricious according to whom? Some bureaucrat? The authors suggest that due process rights are one example of goals imposed on schools that have nothing to do with education at all. Could students be suspended without any chance to explain or defend themselves? On the word of another, anonymous student? Are adults always right and students always wrong?

Would the market-controlled, autonomous schools have to provide English as a second language instruction—one of the more recent higher-order values—or would Hispanic children be admitted but then denied equal opportunity? Would these new public schools have to be handicapped accessible in all programs or would students in wheel chairs be excluded? It's easy to bemoan the huge bureaucratic set of rules, regulations, and restrictions in general and in total as do the authors. When taken apart and examined individually, most are justified and significantly expand the principles of equal opportunity and fairness. Chubb and Moe have not proven their theory that these kinds of democratically imposed, higher-order values are impediments to effective school organization. Even if they had established a correlation, there are some higher-order, Jeffersonian value questions to determine before jumping on the market bandwagon.

On the one hand, Chubb and Moe argue that choice is a cure-all for education: "Without being too literal about it, we think reformers would do well to entertain the notion that choice is a panacea" (p. 217). On the other hand, they suggest:

> We are not claiming, as some critics charge, that our data analysis "proves" our case for educational choice. We stand behind our analysis, but we recognize that nothing is ever proven in social science and that the facts may ultimately show us to be wrong. We therefore welcome debate about the facts. (Chubb and Moe 1991: 19)

Chubb and Moe and all the other political scientists, think-tank researchers, number crunchers, professors, politicians, and corporate executives can "welcome debate" in their ivory towers about experiments and how to fix what may or may not be wrong with all the schools in America. Down here in the trenches, at the broad bottom of the bureaucratic hierarchy, students are choosing, schools are closing, choices are being eliminated, inequities are increasing, and basic institutions fundamental to our democratic heritage are crumbling. It's no debating society down here. What if a decade or so of choice ultimately shows them to be wrong?

5

Choice and Deregulation

"What our schools need is a healthy dose of competition" was the headline of an article in *Business Week* (Becker 1989: 28).

"Competition makes business perform. Choice can do the same for public schools," said David Kearns, former chairman of Xerox and currently U.S. Deputy Secretary of Education (Fierman 1989: 147).

"If a school doesn't have good teaching, it will file for bankruptcy, like any other business, and these are market forces at work," asserts former Minnesota Governor Rudy Perpich (Randall 1991: 158).

"Education has become a service provided bureaucratically by an inefficient government monopoly," states John Brandl (in Nathan 1989: 58).

"Rarely do these plans [enrollment choice] take any steps to free up the supply side by decontrolling," argue Chubb and Moe (Chubb and Moe 1990: 207).

Choice will "probably 'weed out' lackluster schools," predicts Peggy Hunter, enrollment options specialist with the Minnesota Department of Education (Kennedy 1989: 4A).

"Forcing schools to compete for students and money holds the key to unlocking the 'bureaucratic gridlock' that hamstrings public education," maintains Osborne and Gaebler (Olson 1992b: 1).

"Choice works, and it works with a vengeance," prophesied former President Reagan (Bastian 1990: 19).

Competition, bankruptcy, market forces, supply side, decontrol (deregulation), and monopoly are all terms from the private sector, from the discipline of economics. Clearly, choice is the application of economic theory to education. Is it a valid application? The private sector, oversimplifying and overinterpreting "declining" test scores, naively assumes that the introduction of competition will automatically increase performance and productivity in education. It is bad enough that this assumption is unsupported by any research, empirical evidence or reliable data. It is far worse to have forgotten the abuses of competition in business and to have neglected to anticipate similar abuses in education. It is also intellectually dishonest to selectively use only those economic concepts that support choice and ignore those that don't fit the premise.

Chubb and Moe at least admit that markets are not perfect: "Markets are inevitably subject to all sorts of real-world imperfections . . . monopolizing, price-fixing, territorial agreements and other restrictive practices by producers may limit the choices available to consumers" (1990: 34). But, they continue, "It is a mistake, however, to place too much emphasis on these sorts of imperfections, just as it is a mistake to be obsessed with the imperfections of democratic control" (p. 34). Logically then, from their perspective, they leave the acknowledgment of potential market imperfections to one paragraph and spend the next two hundred pages obsessing over the imperfections of democratic control.

Let's examine the imperfections or abuses of the real-world markets and how they might play out in an educational setting. In theory, competitive markets are supposed to benefit consumers by providing a wider variety of choices of higher quality products or services at lower prices. This is predicated on the assumption that consumers have access to the information necessary to make informed choices and are motivated by a desire for better products at lower prices. According to theory, the role of government in a market system is inversely related to the degree of pure competition. The more government involvement, the less competitive the market. The government operates more as an umpire than a player in this game. As Chubb and Moe envision government application of markets to education, "public authority must be put to use in creating a system that is almost entirely beyond the reach of public authority" (p. 218).

An ancient proverb says that history repeats itself. George Santayana expanded the proverb: "Those who cannot remember the past are condemned to repeat it." Those who fail to learn from the mistakes of the past are doomed to repeat them. Perhaps political scientists should brush up on their history before applying laissez-faire economics to the field of education. From what is by now almost ancient history, we learn that it has taken an enormous amount of legislation and judicial involvement to prevent and correct abuses in the market system. While the Sherman Antitrust Act was used by the courts to break up Rockefeller's Standard Oil in 1911 for unreasonable restraint of trade, the Clayton Antitrust Act of 1914 was required to outlaw price discrimination. Foul, cried the umpire. More loopholes were discovered and the Robinson-Patman Act of 1936 was passed to forbid "favored" rebates and discounts that were not available to all buyers of goods. Foul again, cried the umpire.

This thumbnail sketch of robber-barons and trust-busting identifies a history lesson. Competitive markets tend to be self-eliminating and therefore require constant umpiring to re-establish competition and protect consumers. Did we learn the lesson or did we repeat the same mistakes? Enter President Reagan and his entourage. Haynes Johnson describes them as

> self-made men who espoused rugged individualism, free (that is, unfettered and unregulated) enterprise, and a belief in the survival of the fittest. They were Social Darwinists who had made it out of poverty. So could others, if they were worthy. Their maxims were simple ones. . . . Essentially they believed

in no government—or none that would impede their interests (Johnson 1991: 72)

With Reagan's "get government off our backs" theme, we had deregulation and supply-side economics. The supply side of educational choice is deregulation of schools to provide the necessary autonomy and flexibility to be competitive. Before examining how that might work, let's see how the supply-side theories worked in the real world. Did we get a "better mousetrap" of economic theory or a failure to learn the lessons of history?

The standard text definition of supply-side economics is "government policies designed to stimulate the growth of aggregate supply" (Clark and Veseth 1987: 333). This is accomplished by cutting taxes, reducing or eliminating the business costs of government regulation, and creating a more competitive marketplace. In other words, supply-side economics is "taking care of business." If economic policies are implemented to benefit the supply side, those benefits would trickle down to the rest of society. In theory, the increased profits realized by suppliers (business) would be used for increased research and development, capital investment, growth and expansion, the creation of new jobs. The new growth and jobs would then be taxed, resulting in an increase in government revenue: the Laffer curve. Even though Reagan proposed dramatic increases in defense spending along with tax cuts, supply-side economics would overcome this contradictory combination. Reagan predicted that his plan would cut the national debt and produce a surplus after three years (Johnson 1991: 131).

Not everyone was sold on the new supply-side theories in 1980. Economics Professor Robert M. Dunn, Jr., of George Washington University referred to them as "old snake oil in a new bottle." Reagan's opponent for the Republican nomination, George Bush, characterized supply-side economics as "voodoo economics" (Johnson 1991: 104–5). More than a decade later, the question is: Did they work? When Reagan took office in 1981, the national debt was $907.7 billion. When he left office in 1989, the national debt was just under $3 trillion. No surplus, tripled debt—where's the umpire? Fired!

What happened? Contrary to theory, in the real world, suppliers did not plow increased profits back into research and development, expansion, and new jobs. Instead, cashing in and short-term profit-taking became the name of the game. And the game was now being played with few or no umpires. It was "let's make a deal" time, as merger mania rewrote the very language of American business. As *Time* magazine reported in its cover story in a 1985 issue,

> In the heat of a takeover battle, a "white knight" may be summoned to buy a company and rescue it from a corporate raider. Or the target may swallow a "poison pill" by taking a huge load of debt or some other obligation that makes it less attractive. Nearly every company has by now spread "shark repellent" to ward off would-be attackers. (*Time* 1985: 43).

In this game, the end justified the means: "The end was making money, by whatever means it took to achieve it. . . . Ivan Boesky stood up at Harvard [Berkeley] and said, 'Greed is good' " (Johnson 1991: 223, 242). The means included junk bonds, insider trading, "greenmail," leveraged buy-outs, parking stock, dual trading on the futures exchange, stock-index futures, and so on. Some means were legal, some illegal, most unethical, and almost none in the best interests of society. "During the Reagan years the wave of corporate mergers, take-overs and restructuring resulted in more than twenty-five thousand deals, cumulatively valued at more than two trillion dollars" (Johnson 1991: 220). This activity does not produce long-term research and development, capital investment, or new jobs and opportunities. Are we sure we want supply-side deregulation applied to education?

Corporate managers have to be concerned with fighting take-over attempts instead of concentrating on running their companies. Long-term planning is sacrificed to short-term profit-taking in order to maintain stockholders' support against raiders. The volatile corporate changes disrupt communities, throw people out of jobs or force relocation, and devastate morale within the organization. Perhaps the strongest criticism is the fact that mergers and takeovers create mammoth corporate debt. Borrowing to buy companies and borrowing to fight off being bought have saddled corporate America will trillions of dollars in IOUs. "A Wall Street lawyer summed up the argument against mergers and takeovers this way: 'They do not create jobs. They do not add to the national wealth. They merely rearrange ownership interests and shift the risk from shareholders to creditors' " (Wolken and Glocker 1988: 319). Will consolidation be the education version of merger mania?

The airline industry is an interesting example of the consequences of deregulation. In this case, deregulation was supposed to produce more carriers and choices for consumers, better service and lower rates. Initially, there were lots of carriers and fare-wars reduced rates. Between 1978 and 1986, the number of large airlines grew from 43 to 80. There were more than 140 commuter and smaller carriers in operation. However, merger mania took over and the market is now dominated by three mega-carriers and much more concentration than existed before deregulation. Between 1985 and 1988, 24 mergers were allowed and by 1991, 150,000 airline workers were out of work. In December 1991, Pan American Airways suspended operation. TWA has indicated it will seek bankruptcy protection in early 1992 (*Time*, December 16, 1991: 60). By definition, where there are winners, there are losers. According to Alfred Kahn, former Civil Aeronautics Board (CAB) chairman and a major architect of deregulation, the current concentration of airlines "is the fault of the Department of Transportation, which has failed to enforce the nation's antitrust laws" (Wolken and Glocker 1988: 246). That sure sounds like a deregulator asking for more regulation.

The real losers, however, are the consumers and the general public. After ten years, there is less competition, fewer carriers, fewer choices, and higher fares. In December 1991, the fares were lower to fly to Europe than between two points in the United States. Consumers now have a hub-and-spoke system in lieu of the direct flights and convenient travel of the pre-deregulation era. Much more alarming are concerns about the effects of deregulation on commercial air safety.

> On a cold and snowy January evening in 1982, an Air Florida 737 jetliner began taxiing down the runway at Washington, D.C.'s National Airport. The plane never reached its destination. Instead, shortly after takeoff, it slammed into the 14th Street Bridge and plunged into the Potomac River, killing 74 people on board and four people on the ground. An investigation revealed that the tragic crash was, in part, the result of the inexperienced flight crew's failure to exercise good judgment during takeoff procedures. There were more accidents involving airplanes in 1985 than in any previous year in aviation history. (Wolken and Glocker 1988: 242)

Is this another case of cut costs, increase profits? Not so, says American Airlines Chairman Robert Crandall, who argues in favor of continued deregulation. He argues, "The FAA is responsible for safety" (Castro and Woodbury 1991: 18). Some other regulator?

But a blue-ribbon presidential commission on aviation safety assessed the changes wrought as airline deregulation replaced economic regulations and concluded,

> The present governmental structure is not working effectively enough to ensure its safety in the future. . . . Safety improvements have been languishing because of defused authority and accountability. . . . In short, now is the time for decisive action by Congress and the Executive Branch. (Johnson 1991: 172)

But action seems unlikely with Bush's appointment of Samuel Skinner (Federal Aviation Agency administrator who presided over the airline catastrophe) to chief of staff, replacing John Sununu, who had his own variety of airline difficulties. If deregulation has made the skies a little less safe, what might it do to America's schools?

Deregulation has had its impact in the public as well as the private sector. In many respects, the term "deregulation" became a euphemism for the contempt of government and its institutions. The lax enforcement and hands-off approach to regulation allowed a cynicism to spread throughout the federal agencies and conflicts of interest became standard operating procedure. In 1983, Assistant Housing and Urban Development (HUD) Secretary Savas resigned before being fired for "abuse of office." By the spring of 1989, just months into the Bush presidency,

> congressional investigators began documenting abuses at HUD that would cost the taxpayers billions of dollars in losses. Worse, the scandal that unfolded was shown to have been one in which all the normal processes of accountability and oversight within the executive branch, HUD, the Congress, and the press had broken down. In the vacuum that resulted, HUD became the personal vehicle for the rich and politically well connected to exploit low-income housing programs designed to help the poor. (Johnson 1991: 180)

Will deregulated choice have sufficient accountability and oversight to protect schools and students from exploitation?

In 1988, a scandal surfaced again in the defense industry. Laid bare were the lucrative connections among defense contractors, defense consultants, and Pentagon employees.

> Together they formed a U.S. defense industry that was spending $160 million a day on military procurement. Favors, gifts, rigged contracts, trading of inside information, smuggling of classified documents out of Pentagon offices to be passed to military contractors were part of the story. (Johnson 1991: 177)

Senator David Pryor (Democrat, Arkansas) described the period of deregulation, "It has been an eight year feeding frenzy at the

Department of Defense." Worse yet, this happened in spite of the fact that there were repeated warnings that were not acted upon. Reagan himself had received a blunt warning from a blue-ribbon commission he had appointed to examine the defense contract situation. By May 1985 there were 131 investigations pending against 45 of the largest defense contractors: "The cases involved such issues as defective pricing, cost and labor mischarging, substitution of products, subcontractor kickbacks and false claims" (Johnson 1991: 177–78).

Haynes Johnson's book, *Sleepwalking Through History*, includes a thorough and very readable analysis of the consequences of supply-side deregulation. He lists 18 federal agencies, departments, bureaus, or commissions that had ethical problems. By the end of the Reagan administration, 138 administrative officials had been convicted, indicted, or investigated for misconduct and/or criminal violations—a new record. Public service had become another oxymoron. Johnson reports that Reagan's typical response to instances of wrongdoing by aides was to criticize those who brought the charges or blame the media that reported them. "The standard he set and that was followed by many whom he appointed to serve him was not to police or regulate the system; rather, it was to disband and deregulate it. The idea was to let the private market forces work in the public sector" (Johnson 1991: 184–85). That sounds almost word for word like former Minnesota Governor Perpich on choice in education!

The worst was yet to come.

> For more than a decade, official Washington has engaged in a massive cover-up desperately trying to hide the true dimensions of the saving and loan debacle. . . . American taxpayers will have to pay a cleanup bill that could exceed $500 billion by the year 2020. (Roberts and Cohen 1990: 53)

This mess began with deregulation to save the ailing savings and loan industry, created in the 1930s for the worthy purpose of enabling millions of Americans to buy homes on reasonable terms.

A series of deregulations created an environment in which "scores of investors like Charles Keating moved in swiftly, turning the thrift industry into a huge casino where only the taxpayers could lose" (Roberts and Cohen 1990: 55). The huge sums of money involved allowed the thrift industry buccaneers to exert enormous pressure on government officials, from the Keating Five to the Bush administration. By 1986, the cover-up was approaching a conspiracy (Roberts and Cohen 1990: 58).

The Bush campaign in 1988,

> run by James Baker, who had been White House chief of staff and Treasury Secretary as the crisis grew, was determined to keep it off the agenda. Baker had been a key figure in trying to limit the scope of bailout legislation in 1986 and 1987, even as the crisis was growing. In the campaign endgame, he and other GOP officials were instrumental in making sure bailout legislation wasn't discussed until after Bush was elected (Roberts and Cohen 1990: 59).

Donald Regan, primary deregulator and also a former Treasury Secretary and chief of staff, says he has learned that there is an "avaricious, greedy, criminal element" in all industries. If he had known then what he knows now, would he have favored so much deregulation? "The answer is no" (p. 55). The S&L story is one of the most discouraging and depressing I have ever read. And the last chapter will be written by my grandchildren as they pay the bill!

Deregulation has already jeopardized the financial future for generations to come. Do we want to take similar risks with their educational future? Does firing the umpire deregulate to politically appointing the state commissioner or superintendent? What form will merger mania take in the deregulated educational environment of choice? Consolidations, disrupted communities, laid-off and demoralized teachers? What happens to the children when their school goes bankrupt? How do the supply-side benefits "trickle down" to them? With the umpires fired and the safeguards gone, will we see creative, new forms of short-term profit-taking in lieu of long-term investment? Will kickbacks, substitution of products, and false claims surface in text or capital expenditures, athletics, or transportation? What will the educational cover-up look like? Schools-for-profit, not for kids? What exactly will be the new bottom line? "Greed is good," but for schools? Avarice exists in all industries, and education is one of the biggest. The potentials are enormous. When will we learn?

6

Choice and Supply Side

Selectivity and relativity are modi operandi inherent in most advocacies, and the proponents of choice in education fit the MO on many counts. They selectively emphasize those test scores and educational data analyses that help to create the impression of a general crisis in education and squelch those that don't. "Bureaucracy" and "bureaucrat" are names called only those institutions or individuals who question choice and whose only possible motivation is self-interest. From the theories of economics, choice advocates select only those that advance their agenda, ignoring the rest. In addition, the private sector component of the coalition has learned to brandish an economic theory when it's useful and bury it when it becomes inconvenient.

For example, the supply-side dogma of hands-off, laissez-faire economics was the rally cry of the corporate and political support for deregulation. Let the marketplace regulate and determine the fate of business, not government. Sink or swim, it's survival of the fittest. There were no such slogans, however, when the government had to bail out the Chrysler and the Lockheed corporations. In 1984, the government bought a bank to prevent a bankruptcy: "Businesses, including small banks, go bankrupt every day. Continental Illinois, however, was not just another bank. The failure of a bank of this size would have international repercussions" (Wolken and Glocker 1988: 182).

Poor judgment combined with a desire for ever-higher profits had led Continental Illinois to make many high-risk loans for oil and gas exploration and to Latin American countries. This bailout prevented the marketplace payoff for poor judgment. Relatively speaking, it's survival of the fittest, except when weak. The point is not that the bailouts were wrong. On the contrary, their success reaffirms the need for regulation, or re-regulation in some cases. However, the situational use of basic principles is intriguing. In good times, the government should keep out of business, but in bad times, the government better act.

In October 1987, the stock market experienced the worst crash since 1929. By the close on Monday, October 19, stock market prices had dropped 22.6 percent, almost double the record losses in 1929. The Dow-Jones averages fell 508 points. That was Black Monday. On Terrible Tuesday, "the financial system approached breakdown. . . . In that moment of maximum peril the Federal Reserve Board in Washington stepped in forcefully and dramatically, . . . announced its readiness to serve as a source of liquidity to support the economic and financial system" (Johnson 1991: 380–81). While there is still debate over what caused the crash and what precipitated the recovery, in a five-minute period shortly after the Fed announcement, the market rallied by the equivalent of a 360 point Dow-Jones averages increase. The irony was that "in the end what kept '87 from turning into another '29 was the very hand of the federal government that Reagan and the supply-siders had railed against" (Johnson 1991: 386).

The arguments over free trade and protectionism are another interesting study in the relative rhetoric of the private sector. The domestic automobile industry, for example, is loud and clear in its support of supply-side policies, including a hands-off, laissez-faire approach by government or requirements for pollution control, reduced mileage, or increased safety. The industry rhetoric changes diametrically when discussing the domestic sales and market share of Toyota and Honda and the need for government protection and intervention. All of a sudden, the corporate concern for workers' jobs and communities is admirable. The invisible hand becomes visible once again. Will the "real" rhetoric step forward and sign in, please?

Is this hypocrisy? Not if one assumes that the real agenda, the bottom line, is any means necessary to increase profit—as it should be, according to the very basic tenets of market theory. As Adam Smith, author of *The Wealth of Nations*, wrote,

> It is not from the benevolence of the butcher, the brewer, or the baker, that we expect our dinner, but from their regard to their own interest. We address ourselves, not to their humanity, but to their self-love, and never talk to them of our own necessities but of their advantages. Nobody but a beggar chooses to depend chiefly upon the benevolence of his fellow citizens. (Wolken and Glocker 1988: 119)

Profit is the motivation of the market. It's the rhetoric that obscures the motive and confuses us. Are we being similarly confused with the market rhetoric applied to education?

A critical issue in the protectionism versus free trade debate is short-term profits versus long-term gains. Protectionism is a method to increase short-term profits at the expense of long-term increases in innovation, efficiency, and competitiveness. Similarly, educational choice provides a quick-fix, short-term cap on education expenditures, potential reduction in tax burden and the resulting increase in corporate profits, at the expense of long-term equity of opportunity for all students and commitment to the communities they live in. Are we certain that the motivations and methods of the market have a place in education?

In addition to their rhetorical relativity, the selective use of economic principles by proponents to justify enrollment choice in education ignores a significant body of theory that just doesn't fit.

There is both a demand side and a supply side to the issue of educational choice. Both sides require a thorough examination.

> According to Elmore (1988), the demand side asks the question of whether the consumers of education should be given the central role of choosing their education. The supply side of the issue poses the question of whether the suppliers in education should be given the autonomy to respond to the consumers in a flexible way. (First 1991: 5)

Let's not forget, however, that the original supply-siders of the Reagan era had two agendas: to deregulate and cut taxes. Elmore fails to mention the tax cut part, which helps explain the participation by business in the choice coalition. In the next chapter, the demand-side issues of who can choose and the consumer costs of choice will be the focus. For the remainder of this chapter, issues related to the supply side of the choice equation will be examined.

One criterion for a competitive market is the ease of entry of suppliers into the market. With choice introducing market competition into education, how easy is entry into the market? In education, a large percentage of the total start-up costs of providing service are fixed costs, requiring enormous capital investment. The school building itself and the variety of specialized facilities required within the building are significant costs. Those specialized facilities include gymnasiums, showers, washrooms, home economics labs, industrial arts (woodworking, metals, welding, autos), art, music (vocal and instrumental), computer labs, business education labs, libraries, theaters, media centers, science labs, and cafeterias.

According to Chubb and Moe (1990), the bad public schools would fold once people were given a choice, and new, better schools would be founded by entrepreneurs, who would be able to survive economically because of the government "scholarships." However, these scholarships or vouchers provide only operating funds. Where will the kind of capital money come from for these new, entrepreneurial schools to spring up and provide choice? It is hard to imagine that these kinds of costs would not be significant barriers to entry into the market.

Hastening to be first in all things, carefully thought out or not, Minnesota passed legislation for the nation's first "charter schools." "Sponsors argue that, by breaking school boards' monopoly on starting up and running public schools, the new law will be a 'supply side' reform that will expand educational choices for students and free teachers from oppressive rules and regulations," reports Lynn Olson in her article, "Supply Side Reform or Voucher? Charter-School Concept Takes Hold" (Olson 1992a: 1). While the law does not provide for any start-up costs, "it's the most sweeping exemption from the whole book of rules that has ever been put into law," says Ted Kolderie, a leading proponent of the concept (Olson 1992a: 22).

Perhaps "autonomy for flexibility" and "sweeping exemptions" will dictate that the new choice schools will not be required to have the variety of facilities that the public schools have had to provide. According to Chubb and Moe, "The state will have the responsibility for setting criteria that define what constitutes a 'public school' under the new system. These criteria should be quite minimal" (Chubb and Moe 1990: 219). The new choice marketplace of education may end up settling for warehouses and barns or severe limits on the number of competitors. The proponents of choice have simply failed to take buildings and facilities, the "bricks and mortar" issues, into consideration. Perhaps this is by design. It certainly is interesting in light of several recent surveys and studies on the present condition of the nation's school buildings.

A survey by the American Association of School Administrators found that 13,200, or 12 percent, of the nation's public school buildings were inadequate. Old age was the most commonly cited reason for the buildings' poor condition. In all, 74 percent of public schools were built either before World War II or during the 1950s and 1960s to meet the Baby Boom needs. The cost of just catching up on deferred maintenance in public schools has been estimated at $100 billion by the Association of School Business Officials.

"All the talk about national goals, about [President Bush's proposed] 'new American Schools'—it can't be done without changing the facilities," said Tony J. Wall, the executive director of the Council of Educational Facility Planners International.

"We have totally ignored our capital infrastructure—buildings—in our educational thinking," adds architect Franklin Hill (Schmidt 1991: 13). Will the reduction of bureaucratic "bricks and mortar" requirements, deregulation, autonomy for flexibility in the new choice marketplace simply enable society to duck the pending "buildings" bill, the long overdue account?

High capital costs are not the only potential barriers to entry into the choice marketplace. Student transportation has implications on both the demand and supply side of the education choice equation. On the supply side, transportation in a choice marketplace is the antithesis of efficiency, particularly in rural America. Any choice system that purports to be equitable has to require schools to provide student transportation to and from school. Without this requirement, access to choice options will be limited by the families' ability to provide transportation. With Minnesota's open enrollment, we have already seen three buses from different schools meeting at the same intersection. With an equitable interdistrict choice program, transportation will be the epitome of wasted resources, duplicated services, and costly inefficiency.

The public school system in America has been blasted by the proponents of choice as monopolistic. Yet both common sense and economic theory suggest that some monopolies exist for good reason and are natural or logical monopolies. Considering start-up capital costs and transportation for every student, education is most analogous to electricity. Providing efficient service to all consumers, especially those at the end of the line, is logically done by one provider. Even so, whether it's electric cable laid or school buses routed, the marginal cost of service at the end of the line is high. When the capital costs and efficiency requirements are factored in, it seems logical that both electric service and education be treated as natural monopolies. In theory, where natural monopolies exist, government regulation is essential to set prices and establish standards for the quality of service provided. Choice doesn't fit this part of the market theory.

Marginal cost at the end of the line is not the only problem with choice. In fact, the entire field of marginal analysis has been ignored in the rhetoric of choice. On the supply side, in a public choice system like Minnesota's open enrollment, the principles of marginal analysis suggest significant potential for increasing existing inequities between school districts.

Example. In Losing School District 3, the 1989–90 K–12 population of 975 students was reduced by 32 students, who applied for open enrollment or used post-secondary enrollment in a community college for the 1990–91 school year. The loss in revenue for 1990–91 and succeeding years was approximately $150,000. As the administration prepared the board for the necessary reductions, frustrations arose. It was very difficult to make cuts that corresponded or were proportional to the lost revenue. Two of the open enrollment students leaving were in first grade, two in second, one in third, three in fourth, two in fifth, one in sixth, five in seventh, two in eighth, three in ninth, four in tenth, two in eleventh, and one in twelfth. Four students opted for post-secondary enrollment. The average enrollment per grade was 75 students, allowing for three classes or sections of about 25 students each. At no grade level could a section be cut without significantly increasing class size to 35 or more.

Example. In Winning School District 2, 22 of the students from Losing District 3 applied for open enrollment admission for the 1990–91 school year. That was a nice increase in the district's 1989–90 enrollment of 2,350. The increased revenue of approximately $110,000 was pure gravy. Because the grade distribution of the new enrollees was so even, not a single section needed to be added. Instead, the board used the additional revenue to add services like elementary counseling and hire a marketing expert to explore ways to continue the growth pattern in years to come.

The marginal costs to Winning District 2 of educating the new students was as close to zero as were the expenditure reductions to compensate for the marginal revenue lost in Losing District 3.

The dollars per student were the same, but the relative impact (positive or negative) of those dollar transfers was dramatically different in the two districts. Choice provides us with a new twist on windfall profits. This kind of analysis is essential to understanding the consequences of choice. This is a typical, rather than unique, example. Smaller districts frequently have higher per-pupil costs than do larger districts, due to economies of scale.

But the school finance impacts of choice, revealed by marginal analysis, are not confined to small schools. As reported by Julie Underwood, the co-director of the Wisconsin Center for Educational Policy, the Milwaukee choice program, in its second year during 1991–92,

> will reduce state aid to Milwaukee Public Schools by approximately $2.5 million over the school year, with no corresponding reduction in expenditures. Since these students would not come from the same school or program, but from throughout the system, the school district could not expect any reduction in expenditures based on the loss of these students. (Underwood 1991: 18)

As in the case of Losing District 3, all of the students that left were "on the bubble," at the threshold below which cuts could not be made. There were inequities before the competitive choice race began. However, the marginal analysis of the impacts of choice clearly indicates that the inequities only increase. In this race, the starting blocks have not been adjusted for lane advantage and the heats have not been grouped according to qualifying times. Schools don't start the competition on an equal basis, and they don't have equal ability to run the race. There is no "level playing field" here. It's just not a fair race!

7

Choice and Revenue

The terms "equal," "equitable," and "fair" bring us to perhaps the thorniest, most muddled issue on the supply side of educational choice—revenue. In fact, school finance is the Gordian knot of education, with or without choice. Education is funded by taxes. Simplicity ends here. Throughout the country, the largest portion of school revenue comes from state and local government. Federal contributions average between 3 percent and 6 percent. The education revenues that come from state and local governments are raised by a combination of state and local taxes. There are probably fifty different combinations of the sales tax, lottery, personal and corporate income tax, interest, dividend, capital gains tax, and, of course, the local property tax. Herein lies the problem.

The particular mix or formula of taxes that most states use to fund education is called the foundation system. Most foundation programs represent a compromise between the right of local districts to support their own schools to the degree they choose through the local property tax levy and the state's responsibility to lessen or modify the impact of extremes in local property wealth subject to taxation. The "foundation" represents the amount of support guaranteed to local districts regardless of property wealth. If a district is so poor that the property tax levy required by the formula does not raise the foundation aid guaranteed, the state makes up the difference. This sounds fair enough, and is certainly an improvement since the days of almost exclusive reliance on the property tax for school revenue.

However, there are several problems. First, the amount guaranteed, the foundation aid or formula allowance, is typically set at a low or minimum level. The setting is done by politicians who try to avoid use of the "T-word." Second, this minimum guaranteed support covers general education revenue, operating funds. It does not cover capital expenditures for buildings, facilities, and equipment. In most states, these expenditures are covered through additional (above the formula) property tax levies. Property-rich districts have the best facilities. Property-poor districts can barely maintain facilities, let alone build and remodel. In a third instance, many states, like Minnesota, have allowed local districts the prerogative of going to the taxpayers for excess levies to raise additional, discretionary operating funds above the foundation guarantee. This again works to the advantage of property-rich districts. If the property valuation is high, a small levy raises lots of money. In a property-poor district, extremely high levies would be required to raise the same dollars.

As succinctly described by Jonathan Kozol, these disparities resulting from reliance on the property tax are frequently compounded in the large cities and inner city school districts by the disproportionate number of tax-free institutions, such as colleges, hospitals, and museums, which are located within the cities.

> In some cities, according to Jonathan Wilson, former chairman of the Council of Urban Boards of Education, 30 percent or more of the potential tax base is exempt from taxes, compared to as little as 3 percent in the adjacent suburbs. Suburbanites, of course, enjoy the use of these nonprofit, tax-free institutions; and, in the case of private colleges and universities, they are far more likely to enjoy their use than are the residents of the inner cities. (Kozol 1991: 55)

In addition to the traditionally tax-exempt institutions, economic development packages in recent years have added a confusing overlay of property tax-break incentives to lure corporate investment.

Choice programs force increased dependence on the inequitable property tax. Milwaukee public schools lost $2.5 million in state aid as a result of choice. "The school district, therefore, raised its property tax levy by $2.5 million this year to account for the decline in state aid and the increase in required expenditures" (Underwood 1991: 18). In many cases, enrollment choice will initiate hidden but significant tax shifts from the more equitable, progressive state corporate and personal income taxes to the local property taxes—and this will increase inequity.

Over and over, the rhetoric for choice has included the concept that more money won't help solve the crisis. Chubb and Moe find, "Half of all high performance schools have above-average economic resources, . . . the most dramatic differences between families of high and low performance schools are in income and education, . . . [and] 70 percent of the high performance schools have student bodies above average in SES [socioeconomic status]" (Chubb and Moe 1990: 104, 106, 111). However, they conclude,

> In fact, the relationship between resources and performance has been studied to death by social scientists, and their consistent conclusion has been that resources do not matter much, except perhaps in the cases of extreme deprivation or gross abundance (Chubb and Moe 1990: 193).

The ultimate non sequitur! "Extreme" and "gross" are precisely the issue. Perhaps Chubb and Moe had better read Kozol or take a few field trips.

The disparities of resources and opportunities between rich and poor schools described in Kozol's *Savage Inequalities* are heartbreaking. Anyone reading at this point who has not read Kozol should do so. How can this extreme level of injustice and inequality exist in the world's richest country? Apparently, choices have been made all along, all across the country, for the freedom of the local communities to fund their own schools. When these systems are challenged or questioned, one hears the same kind of "me and mine first" rhetoric of choice and a similarly cynical and callous disregard for the quality of educational opportunity for others. " 'It doesn't make sense to offer something that most of these urban kids will never use,' a businessman said to me flatly in Chicago. 'No one expects these ghetto kids to go to college. Most of them are lucky if they're even literate' " (Kozol 1991: 76).

In the Supreme Court of New Jersey, defendants arguing for the property tax system of school finance stated, "Education currently offered in these poorer ... districts is tailored to the students' present need" and "these students simply cannot benefit from the kind of vastly superior course offerings found in the richer districts" (Kozol 1991: 170). Nevertheless, the Supreme Court called for a systemic remedy, setting off a storm of controversy over any plan to redistribute the resources. "Taking state money from the towns that have high property values to prop up the urban schools," says one letter-writer, "will bring mediocrity to every classroom in the state."

"Putting more money into the poor districts," says another letter-writer, "won't change anything. . . . Money is not the answer. . . . It has to begin in the home." The contempt for the capacities of urban children is particularly ironic when juxtaposed with the prediction of the imminent demise of education in the richer districts if their funding is cut back. "Money, the message seems to be, is crucial to rich districts but will be of little difference to the poor" (Kozol 1991: 170–71).

Since 1971, when the first school finance court case was handed down, more than 35 states have had litigation involving similar issues on school finance. In the District Court of Shawnee County, Kansas, Judge Terry Bullock wrote in October 1991, "For a sobering look at what happens in places where the guarantees of the Kansas Constitution, as announced in this opinion, are not available or not yet observed, see *Savage Inequalities* by Jonathan

Kozol" (Pipho, 1991c: 271). On December 17, 1991, a Minnesota District Court ruled that several provisions of the state's school funding system were unconstitutional: "What is unconstitutional is the unequal capability of school districts to access discretionary revenues due to property-wealth differences, which is the under-lying cause of a system which is not uniform" (*Education Week*, January 8, 1992: 36). This ruling found violations of both the education and equal protection clauses of the Minnesota constitution.

Currently, more than twenty states have court cases on school finance pending (Pipho 1991c: 271). These supply-side, school finance equity issues need to be carefully examined in view of the speed and horsepower of the choice bandwagon. Writing for the North Central Regional Educational Laboratory, Van D. Mueller stated:

> Along with less than fair and adequate general education funding systems, choice is being considered and implemented in states where capital outlay and debt service funding systems are inadequate and unfair. The historic reliance on the property tax to finance school facilities and equipment accompanied by a minimal level or total absence of state funding results in a real dilemma if students are relocating from school district to school district. The unfairness of the current system is simply exacerbated. (Mueller 1991: 16)

Kozol is also highly critical of school-choice proposals, which, he maintains, "will widen the gap between the haves and the have-nots" (Olson, 1991b: 11). Affluent opponents of "Robin Hood" proposals to redistribute educational resources and resolve equity issues are easy to criticize as self-protective and selfish. But as Kozol points out, "They do not want poor children to be harmed, they simply want the best for their own children" (Mitchell 1991: 61). So it is with the proponents of choice. They do not intend to hurt the students who don't or can't choose; they simply want what's best for their own children. "Unintentional" or "inadvertent" are irrelevant adjectives to the inner city, ghetto children suffering the consequences of inequity. Will they also be irrelevant to the consequences of choice for our public schools?

With the supply side of choice advocacy and implementation swiftly broadening from public school choice to include charter schools, private schools, religious schools, vouchers, deregulation, and sweeping exemptions from rules and regulations, one wonders if there is any intent in this restructuring to maintain the public school system at all. The supply-side marketplace depends on the competition of the suppliers, with only the fittest surviving. How can the public schools continue to compete and survive when everyone else in the business will play by different and far less costly rules? Do we extend similar deregulation to all public schools? With what consequences, and for whom? When a more complete range of market concepts is considered and the complexity of taxation and school finance is factored in, the choice issues are nowhere near as simple as the rhetoric suggests. The long-term effects set in motion need to be logically and thoroughly thought through and anticipated.

Choice is clearly about economics applied to education, and much of economics is simply common sense and logic applied to human behavior. However, economics, like any field of behavioral analysis, is subject to some common logical errors, fallacies, and omissions. In the choice application of economic theory to education, several errors and omissions have crept in that invalidate the conclusions. A glaring theoretical omission is the failure to consider the concepts of externalities and public goods. In competitive market theory, consumers get the full benefit of their purchases and the suppliers bear the full cost of their production decisions. This means there are no externalities or public goods. "Markets break down when externalities and public goods appear. The market's invisible hand makes mistakes" (Clark and Veseth 1987: 693).

Externalities are defined as costs or benefits of a decision imposed on others not party to the decision. Externalities are also referred to as spill-over effects or neighborhood effects. Choice certainly fits the definition. When students exercise choice, the rest of the resident school community pays. Markets work best when involved in the exchange of private goods. Private goods are items that display the characteristics of rivalry and exclusion. Rivalry exists when one's use of a good or service diminishes the amount available for others; exclusion means that an individual owner or consumer of a good or service can exclude others from its benefits. Education is clearly a public good, displaying neither rivalry nor exclusion. "Markets undersupply public goods because individuals have the incentive to be free riders, to let others buy, then gain costless benefits. Much less education might be produced and consumed, with detrimental effects, if government let educational markets alone" (Clark and Veseth 1987: 701–5).

The Clark and Veseth college economics text outlines the common logical errors that can plague behavioral analysis. One is called the fallacy of composition, the incorrect belief that what is true for the individual is also true for the entire group (p. 33). This fallacy is so common in the choice rhetoric that it needs little clarification. A choice works for one student here and there, and therefore all students should have choice for any reason. Microeconomics studies individual choices; macroeconomics studies the aggregate effects. Choice proponents have left out the macroeconomics component altogether.

Another common error in logical and economic analysis is post hoc reasoning, the conclusion that the chronological order in which events occur is related to the cause and effect of those events. It incorrectly assumes that correlation implies causation. Classic examples of post hoc reasoning are found in the working papers prepared by the Minnesota House of Representatives Research Department for the evaluation of open enrollment. If a high school offers Russian and a lot of elementary students choose to transfer into that district, then Russian is desirable? Choice is working?

A third error in reasoning is ignoring secondary effects. Any cause-and-effect relationship can have both direct and secondary effects. "Secondary effects are the results of an initial action that are realized over time, often having the opposite effect of that action and frequently being of much greater importance" (Clark and Veseth 1987: 34). The time frame, the long run, is the critical issue in secondary effects. This becomes crucial when considering that decisions about choice will be made by politicians. Clark and Veseth describe the shortsightedness that occurs when politicians are making economic decisions. The terms of office for most politicians range from two to four years. The lag between the time that an economic action is taken and the point at which its full secondary effects are felt can often be longer than a term of office. Planning horizons for politicians seldom, if ever, exceed their term of office.

> The shortsightedness effect can be summed up with the following axioms: The greater the short-run benefits and the clearer and more obvious those benefits are to voters, the more likely politicians are to vote for such an issue. The more long term the costs of an economic action and the more difficult it is for voters to identify those costs, the more likely politicians are to vote for such a bill. . . . The nature of the political system therefore makes it difficult for politicians to consider the long-run economic problems of the economic systems as thoroughly as they might consider more short-term problems. (Clark and Veseth 1987: 123)

There is little evidence that any consideration of the long-range effects of choice have been a part of the public debate or political consideration. In five or ten years, what will the effect be on the children who can't choose to leave the inner city schools, the disabled and special education students who will have no place in the newly deregulated market schools, the rural communities that have lost their schools to the hidden agendas of consolidation and "bigger is better"?

The Massachusetts experience with choice is a classic example of what happens when laws are passed without thorough consideration of spill-over or secondary effects. "The Massachusetts legislature's joint education committee has voted to repeal the state's controversial school-choice law that was hastily adopted during the budget process last year" (Diegmueller 1992: 17). According to one state legislator, "It was a rob-Peter-to-pay-Paul scenario. Communities were making decisions purely for economic reasons and not for educational reasons" (Diegmueller 1992: 17). "To ease some of the financial stress, the legislature late last year appropriated $2.4 million in emergency aid to school districts that had been penalized when their students elected to take advantage of the school-choice program and attend other districts" (Diegmueller 1992: 17). It was estimated that the cost of this student/dollar transfer would rise to between $15 and $25 million if the law was not changed. In addition, the law "tended to benefit children from white, middle-income families, many of whom had already been sending their children to out-of-district schools and paying tuition on their own" (Diegmueller 1992: 17). Choice can create more problems than it solves.

Perhaps the most intriguing and applicable description of a fallacy of logic in economics is found in Herman Daly and John Cobb's 1989 book, *For the Common Good*. The book is a significant critique of traditional economic methods and theories and offers new insight into the concepts of externalities and long-term secondary effects mentioned above. The book has a general perspective that is important to the consideration of choice in education. The specific concept of interest here is called the fallacy of misplaced concreteness. Daly and Cobb discuss the mathematization of economics, the only social science awarded the Nobel prize. They state, "Economists have developed the habit of dressing up their rather imprecise ideas in the language of the infinitesimal calculus. . . . Any pretense of applying precise formulae is a sham and a waste of time" (Daly and Cobb 1989: 31).

Read an example from Chubb and Moe's work.

Appearances, however, can be deceiving. The importance of a regression coefficient, once it is found to be significant, cannot be determined by any single statistical standard. If we interpret the unstandardized regression coefficients—the first coefficients listed for each variable in table 4-8—the influences on student achievement take on new meaning and greater importance" (Chubb and Moe 1990: 128).

Examine a criticism of their work. Anthony S. Bryk, Associate Professor of Education at the University of Chicago,

> agreed that he has "problems with" their equation that links school organization with student performance. They put all the tests together and control for tracking. It's far from clear their omnibus organizational variable can account for it. (Rothman 1990: 20)

The problem in this fallacy of misplaced concreteness is the degree of mathematical abstraction from the real world. As Daly and Cobb suggest:

> Too often economics has shaped its anthropology and its theories with an eye to "analytical convenience" rather than empirical warrant. As a result, policy decisions are determined by mathematical theorems whose virtue is their deductive fruitfulness rather than their connection to the real world. The abstraction has gone too far, and the practitioners of the discipline are too little aware of it. The fallacy of misplaced concreteness is too pervasive. (Daly and Cobb 1989: 95–96)

The relevance of Daly and Cobb's 1989 perceptions to Chubb and Moe's 1990 work on choice is remarkable. If the chronology were right, and the fallacy of post hoc reasoning had not already been discussed, it might be suggested that one book was written in response to the other. Nevertheless, it is disturbing to realize that the education of our children and our grandchildren is being determined based on such serious errors and omissions in logic and reason.

The most serious omission is the obvious. All of the theory and rhetoric of marketplace competition, the abstract models, place a premium on the concept of winners and losers. It is essential to bring the abstractions down to the real world, to focus the obscurity and to put human faces on the actual winners and losers. In the next chapter, real people will be factored into the equations, and we will meet some of the winners and losers.

8

Choice and Demand Side

> Economics is all about how people make choices. Sociology is all about why they don't have any choices to make. (Heath 1976: 3)

Choices are all about information: access to it, relevance and timeliness of it, accuracy and validity of it, source and integrity of it. We have already discussed the choices being made in education and the concerns about the informational base for those decisions. That, however, is more about political science. Information in the economic sense is basic to the operation of a competitive marketplace. Consumers have to have information about the choices available in any marketplace. Informed choices are like votes, sending signals about the amount and quality of the product desired. If consumers make poorly informed choices, they may be encouraging producers to put out shoddy products. The quality of consumer choices is determined by the time and energy consumers put into gathering information and by the quality of the information.

Information sounds like such an innocuous component of the market model. As long as so much of the justification and rhetoric for market choices in education is coming from the private and political sector, let's examine their grades on an information report card. Perhaps we'll find some lessons from history. On the private side, recent Wall Street scandals have led to several indictments and convictions for the abuse of information. That's what insider trading is—the abuse of information. It is the misuse of advance knowledge, confidential information, material non-public knowledge. It is unethical and illegal because it erodes the foundation of a competitive market—essentially equal access to equal information by all consumers. That's why public authorities with fiscal responsibilities, like school boards, are bound by so many requirements regarding the awarding of contracts: public announcements, published specifications, sealed bids, absolute timelines, and so on. Information is a most powerful factor in determining market outcomes, peoples' choices, and human behavior. That's why abuse of information is so tempting. The private side gets an F on the information report card. How does the political side score?

Using and misusing information to influence decisions and behavior can be a high-stakes operation. President Bush has benefited so often from this kind of informational abuse that one has to question his detachment from the basic operations, despite his denials. In his 1988 presidential campaign, "he used the image of Willie Horton, a black convict who raped a white woman while on furlough, to paint Democrat Michael Dukakis as soft on crime" (Goodgame 1991: 45). Crime was the issue, but black and white was the image, over and over again. The latent appeal to racism by the Bush operation was bad enough but

> they knew that as governor Michael Dukakis personally had nothing to do with letting Horton out on a weekend pass. They knew, too, that Dukakis was not even responsible for setting up the furlough program in his state; the Massachusetts furlough program had been established by Dukakis's Republican gubernatorial predecessor. (Johnson 1991: 400)

During the summer of 1991, Thurgood Marshall retired from the Supreme Court. Bush appointed Clarence Thomas to fill the vacancy. Supporters of Clarence Thomas's nomination put together a negative and derogatory television ad, portraying the Democratic senators on the Judiciary Committee as unfit to make such a decision: "Not coincidentally, the ad was produced by the same people who launched the 1988 Willie Horton spot that branded Michael Dukakis soft on crime but left George Bush open to charges of racism" (*Time*, September 16, 1991: 27). This ad was done without Bush's direction or approval, according to the administration. In fact, Bush requested that the ads be pulled off the air, which only heightened the interest in further analysis and expanded television exposure. The images moved from paid political ads in limited markets to free and broad national news coverage. Direct involvement, maybe not; indirect benefit, no question.

In early 1992, evidence surfaced of yet another example of Bush's agendas being advanced by the repeated use of unsubstantiated, emotional, manipulated and purchased "information." In December 1991, as Congress held hearings on the Gulf War resolution, shocking testimony of Iraqi brutality was given by a young Kuwaiti girl. She claimed to have been present at a Kuwaiti hospital and to have witnessed Iraqi soldiers taking babies from incubators and leaving them on the floor—"scattering them like firewood across the floor," said Bush. In cultivating support for the war, Bush referred to this testimony at least ten times in the weeks that followed. The vote for the war resolution passed by five votes in the Senate, and six senators referred to the girl's testimony in justifying their affirmative votes.

In January 1992, ABC's "20/20" and CBS's "60 Minutes" carried stories raising serious questions about the credibility and motivation of the girl's congressional testimony. Her name had not been released originally, to protect her and her family. But, it turns out, she is the daughter of the Kuwaiti ambassador to the United States and a member of the royal family, most of whom were safely and comfortably out of Kuwait by that time.

The public relations firm of Hill and Knowlton, headed at the time by Craig Fuller, former chief of staff to George Bush

when he was Vice President, helped to package and rehearse
the young woman's appearance on behalf of their client,
Citizens for a Free Kuwait, an exile organization primarily
funded by the Emir of Kuwait. . . . Her story had, in fact, been
rehearsed before video cameras by Hill and Knowlton. But
according to Kuwaiti doctors interviewed by "20/20" and "60
Minutes," no such incident had occurred. (Lieberman 1992:
11–12)

The campaign spent over $12 million to shape American opinion.
Activities included not only rehearsing the girl's testimony, but
also using focus groups and lie-detector technology to identify the
emotional triggers that would best persuade the American people
to go to war.

At the time of this writing, there is no evidence that Bush was
involved directly or even aware of these activities. Once again,
however, his agendas were served by the repeated use of bad
information, developed by someone else. In this case, the stakes
were as high as they get. One expects better judgment from the
president and his administration in selecting and emphasizing the
information used to lead the American people in harm's way.
When the decision is war, the president and his administration have
the supreme responsibility to protect the public from this kind of
manipulated misinformation rather than to use it. This is the same
president and administration who "informs" us that there is a
general crisis across the land in education, and choice is the new,
national imperative.

Inside and misused information is not the only informational
problem for consumers to be wary of. The marketing and advertising industry cranks out an enormous amount and variety of
information. The primary purpose is not to inform, however, but
to influence choices. It is generally understood that any information provided is manipulated to serve that primary purpose. In fact,
most high school civics and economics texts have sections on
analyzing such advertising gimmicks and techniques as card stack-
ing, testimonials, bandwagon, plain folks, glittering generalities,

transfer and "bait-and-switch." *Caveat emptor* is always defined as a Latin phrase meaning "let the buyer beware." The implication is that the risk and consequences of believing the information and choosing accordingly are solely the consumers'. This is standard economics, nothing new or remarkable here; it goes with the consumer's freedom of choice in buying a used car, a VCR, a toothbrush. But how does it play in Peoria, where parents are choosing their child's school?

What if the information provided to the consumers in the new educational marketplace is not designed to inform but to increase enrollment? According to Ruth Randall, former state commissioner of education in Minnesota, "Students who move to other schools will soon know whether there is truth in marketing" (Randall and Geiger 1991: 113). That might be a little late for parents and students who choose a new school and discover they did not get what they bargained for. Somewhat callous *caveat emptor*!

A common example is school districts' glossy publications advertising the "Course Offerings Grades 10–12." This listing includes any and all courses that have ever been offered to students in an initial registration period. Only a small fraction of the courses listed will ever appear on the actual schedule. This trick is understood by insiders, but parents and students choosing a new school may be surprised. They make their choice based on the list of course offerings. When they complete final registration for classes, some months later, they discover that most of the choices have been eliminated. "Low registrations," they're told. "Pick something else." This is the educational variety of "bait-and-switch."

Any school marketing brochure that makes reference to test scores would require a significant level of sophistication for consumers to examine critically before choosing. The variety of ways to manipulate test scores is endless.

These include designating large numbers of low-scoring students for placement in special education so that their scores won't "count" in the school reports, retaining students in grade so that their relative standing will look better on "grade-equivalent" scores, excluding low-scoring students from admission to "open-enrollment" schools, and encouraging low-scoring students to drop out. (Darling-Hammond 1991: 223)

Researchers have found widespread "engineering" of student populations in a study of a large urban school district that used performance standards to determine school-level rewards and sanctions (Darling-Hammond 1991: 223). Choice will only increase the emphasis on "high-stakes" testing and encourage new and creative ways of engineering the results.

Ironically, a major obstacle to the functional role of information in the choice model may be the language of education itself. As Anne C. Lewis, a journalist critical of educators for unnecessarily obscure language, points out,

Of course, other professions have their own exclusive languages as well; few of us are privy to the technical vocabularies of lawyers and physicians. But education ought to be in the business of communicating well to everyone. More than any other sector, education should tell clearly and compellingly what it is about. (Lewis 1991: 573)

This is even more important in an education marketplace. A classic example of the obscurity problem is provided by a Minnesota school district marketing its wares for open enrollment.

The school district has produced simple flyers that are distributed with every take-out order by the local McDonald's, the only McDonald's serving customers from ten surrounding communities. First on the list of the school district's descriptions is "implementation of Outcome-Based Education (OBE)." What is OBE, asks the potential parent or consumer. Outcome-based education involves restructuring, requiring a pivotal paradigm shift and a transformational OBE design process. "Design down and deliver up" is the process. Students progress through a series of rubrics and the five-tiered OBE success pyramid includes, from top down, Paradigm, Purposes, Premises, Principles and Practices. Several other catchy and alliterative examples are available from Dr. William Spady's overheads, which are used to train the teachers in this "new and improved" educational innovation. Ironically, the first of four principles of OBE is clarity of focus. If this impenetrable jargon from the latest commercial gurus of reform and restructuring seems to lack clarity or is intimidatingly obscure, imagine its effectiveness in the inner city.

Why such emphasis on the informational part of the market model? It is a key factor in real consumer choice. Whether shopping for an automobile or a school, consumers need to examine different makes and models, compare prices and benefits, evaluate promotional information carefully.

> Gathering this information takes time and effort, and at some point in your shopping it is in your self-interest to stop doing research. You have to consider whether an additional day spent looking at automobiles and gathering information about them is going to save you enough in costs to warrant your expenditure of the additional time and effort. You must make the search decision at the margin. (Clark and Veseth 1987: 28)

In the market model, the time and effort to choose must be considered a scarce resource. Do some parents and students have more of that scarce resource to spend at the margin of educational choice?

Choice advocates respond to this question and concern by attacking the questioner. In a *New York Times* interview, John F. Chubb accused such worriers of "really saying that poor people were 'too stupid' to pick their own schools" (Lemann 1991: 104). Joe Nathan argues that those critics who feel that "although affluent parents may be able to choose what's best for their children, many poor and minority people can't. This is not only arrogant and patronizing, but untrue" (Nathan 1983: 140). These responses may be rhetorically clean put-away shots, but they will certainly seem facile, uncritical, and intellectually dishonest to anyone who has read Kozol's book.

> Bleeding gums, impacted teeth and rotting teeth are routine matters for the children I have interviewed in the South Bronx. Children get used to feeling constant pain. They go to sleep with it. They go to school with it. . . . Children live for months with pain that grown-ups would find unendurable. (Kozol 1991: 20–21)

The grown-ups who want to "empower" these students and families with educational choice had better get out of their ivory towers and visit the South Bronx. These families are not even empowered to choose a dentist. Choices are made within the context of daily life. When entire lives are lived on the margin, where does choosing a school fit into the information as a scarce resource part of the market model? "Is it really so ridiculous to worry that these same parents might fail to become the tough, savvy, demanding education consumers the instant they obtain the right to decide which school gets their children's tuition money" (Lemann 1991: 104).

It is particularly disappointing to be characterized as arrogant and patronizing by people with the academic credentials of Chubb and Nathan. Are the theories and abstract models so disconnected from reality that real people don't factor in? Does academic and professional objectivity pale in the limelight of popular advocacy? Have their hypotheses become so egocentric that such scholars have to engage in defensive name-calling rather than examine all the evidence?

In a doctoral dissertation for Columbia University, "The Sociology of School Choice: A Study of Black Students' Participation in a Voluntary Transfer Plan," Amy Stuart Wells has included a comprehensive review of the existing research on the relationship between socioeconomics and access to information in a school choice model. In an article discussing their 1978 Rand Corporation study of the Alum Rock voucher demonstration project, Bridge and Blackmun concluded, "that a dynamic, constantly changing educational market tends to increase information imperfections, which occur most often among socially disadvantaged groups."

Elmore wrote in 1986, "Deregulated parental choice and competition between schools could quite conceivably have a negative impact on the decision-making ability of those parents who lack information and market power."

In 1974, Mann cited several studies that conclude that the general public lacks information about how schools operate. "This lack of information," said Mann, "is especially acute for lower-income parents who spend large amounts of time satisfying their families' material needs" (Wells 1991: 62–64).

Wells (1991: 67) found that "the majority of the evidence on parents and students' access to information concerning school choice plans demonstrate that low-income and minority families are at a disadvantage." However, even more disturbing than the evident informational obstacles to effective school choice for low-income consumers is a substantial body of social science research suggesting additional barriers. Wells describes several studies documenting such variables as feelings of alienation, powerlessness, and fatalism; external control beliefs; low expectations; and self-deprecation. Wells concludes that a review of the research and literature on the chooser in school-choice options

> has demonstrated ways in which feelings of alienation and powerlessness, feelings of inferiority or separatism as the result of being dominated, or feelings of low expectations and resistance all work as self-inflicted handicaps resulting in unequal competition between members of certain racial and SES groups. (Wells 1991: 97)

So what? Even if there are suspicious omissions in the evidence considered by proponents, what harm could choice do in the inner city schools and students? How could they get any worse? Let's examine. In the first place, choice is a smokescreen, a convenient diversion and delay in facing the tough and controversial issues of equitable reallocation of resources to the inner city. "You don't rearrange the deck chairs on the Titanic," said the chief executive officer of Citicorps Savings of Illinois (Kozol 1991: 80). Second, choice is being offered in lieu of adequate funding necessary to improve the lives and opportunities of poor children. "Money," writes the *Wall Street Journal*, "doesn't buy better education. . . . The evidence can scarcely be better" (Kozol 1991: 133).

But money hasn't been tried equally in all schools, or the state courts wouldn't be having such a field day with school finance. Money would buy a textbook for each child in class in Camden, repair flooding sewers that force regular school closings in East St. Louis, or move classrooms out of closets in Brooklyn. As Kozol relates, a principal from Camden, speaking in the neighboring, affluent community of Princeton, said,

> "If you don't believe that money makes a difference, let your children go to school in Camden. Trade with our children— not beginning in high school. Start when they're little, in the first or second grade." When I say this, people will not meet my eyes. They stare at the floor. (Kozol 1991: 145)

A business leader in Washington, D.C., after a sobering visit to compare city and suburban schools, said, "If anybody thinks that money's not an issue, let the people in Montgomery County put their children in the D.C. schools. Parents in Montgomery would riot" (Kozol 1991: 184). Choice hurts most because it diverts national attention from the real crisis.

9

Choice and Winners
versus Losers

Even worse than providing a convenient substitute for equitable and adequate funding to the inner cities, a cover for the lack of courage and compassion, choice will make the existing terrible situation in the inner city schools much worse. The deregulatory component of choice could rob disadvantaged students of what little hope they have.

> Another possibility—a likelihood in my view—is that a lot of diploma mills would spring up in the ghettos to cash in on the new availability of government tuition stipends. Released from all but the most rudimentary certification and accredit-ation requirements, these schools would be free to be bad— possibly even worse than the schools they supplemented or replaced. (Lemann 1991: 104)

It could never happen, say proponents of choice. Yet something very similar did happen in the Milwaukee voucher plan. "One of the 10 participating private schools—Juanita Virgil Academy— withdrew from the program halfway through the first year, and later went out of business" (Olson 1991d: 12).

According to John Witte, a researcher from the University of

Wisconsin at Madison, "Parents at the school had complained about transportation problems, a shortage of books and materials, overcrowded classrooms, dirty facilities, and a lack of discipline" (Olson 1991d: 12). The school goes out of business, students are out on the street. Of course, new rules and regulations will be developed to see that this doesn't happen again, unless they follow Chubb's advice to avoid such bureaucratic regulations and protect school autonomy.

Kozol leaves no doubt that school segregation is alive and well in our country. Wells reviewed several studies that suggest there are sociological factors present in both the black and white populations that indicate choice will only increase the separateness of our schools and society. For example, in a 1988 study of school choice in Syracuse, N.Y., Maddaus found the overriding factor in choice of school was not learning, but "moral values" and location, and that such concerns "are often proxies for racist and classist attitudes towards schools with poor and minority students" (Wells 1991: 74). He also found "that physical location of a school was most important to low-income people who did not have cars and wanted to be able to walk to the school in case of problems or emergency" (Wells 1991: 74). In a more recent 1990 study, Moore and Davenport found that in four large, urban school districts, magnet schools enrolled a disproportionate number of non-minority students, leaving neighborhood schools more segregated than ever (Wells 1991: 10). "Magnet" refers to selected public schools in large districts that allow elective, district-wide enrollment of students as opposed to the neighborhood public schools where enrollment is determined by residency and geographic boundaries.

Magnet schools were the choice solutions of many large cities to the dual problems of white flight and desegregation orders. Skimming, sorting, and shifting are the terms used to describe the magnet process. In Chicago, a principal describes the magnet schools: "They attract the more sophisticated families, and it leaves us with less motivated children" (Kozol 1991: 47).

The *Chicago Tribune* reported that the magnet system is "a private school system . . . operated in the public schools. Very poor children, excluded from this system," said the *Tribune*, "are 'even more isolated' as a consequence of the removal of the more successful students from their midst" (Kozol 1991: 59).

In Milwaukee, Witte found that the inner city parents who enrolled their children in the private school voucher program "were already more active in the children's learning at home and at school than the average Milwaukee parent" (Olson 1991d: 12).

A Jackson district resident in New York describes the selective admissions process as "a citywide skimming policy that we compare to orange juice—our black youngsters are being treated like the sediment" (Kozol 1991: 108).

Choice is nothing new. It has been around for years in one form or another. The evidence clearly suggests that concerns about the consequences of expanded, nationwide choice on inner-city children are anything but arrogant and paternalistic. It is clear that choice in the inner city will place additional drains on already inadequate and inequitable fiscal resources. It will also drain these schools and communities of a precious human resource, the highest motivated and achieving students with the most involved parents. The concentration and proportion of the most at-risk children will be increased in the poorest schools, which will have even fewer resources to work with. After reviewing over 140 sources of research and literature and conducting her own study of the St. Louis choice system, Wells concludes,

> A laissez-faire policy of choice in which there are choosers and non-choosers, in which education dollars follow students from one school to the next, in which the desires of the individual are emphasized over the needs of the society as a whole, will only serve as a fine-tuned sorting machine. (Wells 1991: 319)

Either the choice advocates and policymakers have been extremely short-sighted in their failure to consider the impact of race and class on school choices, or they don't care, or there are other, less innocent motives. Which is it? Could it be a very cynical and callous move to skim the best and write off the rest? Is it a last-ditch attempt to avoid paying the bill for all children? What if the concerns raised above prove to be accurate after ten or fifteen years of choice? If we are unwilling to pay the bill now, imagine the tab in the future. The savings and loan bill will be insignificant by comparison.

Choice is about winners and losers. Inner-city schools and children, who have been consistent losers in the competition for America's resources, will lose even more in the next round of school choice. The experience with choice in Minnesota indicates that there will be losers in rural America as well as in the inner city. The impact of choice on small towns and rural areas will demonstrate that the problems of poverty are not exclusively those of the inner city, just as the concerns discussed in this section regarding disabled students, abused children and communities are relevant to the large urban areas.

Example. Emily is a very bright, high-achieving student finishing her sophomore year of high school in a small community. Her graduating class will be fewer than thirty students in June 1994. Emily has moved through all of the math and science courses available in her school and would like to use PSEO or open enrollment to gain access to more challenging academic courses, either at a community college or a larger high school, both located in a neighboring city twenty-five miles away. Emily's mother is a single parent and works at a local highway diner. The family's resources are extremely limited and Emily is needed at home after school and evenings to babysit for her younger brother when her mother works. While Emily would qualify for the low-income transportation reimbursement, there is nothing to reimburse because the family has no car.

In this case, where choice would have been exercised for the purpose of academic enrichment, the combination of geography and low income prevent the choosing. It is simply a myth to suggest that choice will be for everyone.

On the other hand, some choices will be exercised that put children at additional risk.

Example. In the fall of 1990, Peter was a new, open-enrollment student in the seventh grade at a good-sized secondary school, with over eight hundred students in grades seven to twelve. He arrived on the first day of school to register, but his records didn't follow for two months. He was scheduled into the regular seventh-grade schedule of required classes. By the fifth week of school, his poor attendance was drawing attention from the counselor and the principal. In addition, the physical education teacher reported to the school nurse that he had seen lots of bruises on the boy. The nurse and counselor both questioned the boy about attendance and the bruises, but got mostly silence. Calls to the previous school district for Peter's records indicated that they had been misplaced in the transfer between their elementary and secondary schools, and the process slowed down. When the records finally arrived, the counselor became even more concerned. Peter had only been enrolled at the previous school for half the year, arriving just after Christmas. His attendance had been poor there as well, and a note from the sixth-grade teacher indicated that a referral had been made to social services at the end of May. It wasn't until after Thanksgiving 1990 that the counselor and principal had enough of the puzzle pieces assembled to proceed. When Peter's parents were finally reached in mid-December to come in for a conference, they said it wouldn't be necessary because the family was breaking up and Peter would be going to live with an aunt in a neighboring community in another county. A call was made to social services requesting some follow-up, and the case was closed.

Was Peter an abused child? The increased mobility afforded abusive parents by open enrollment makes answering that question even more difficult. The public schools are a primary source of child abuse and neglect referrals. Investigating these kinds of problems is never easy. Open enrollment makes it even more difficult and increases the chances that those children most at risk will fall through the gaping holes in the safety net.

Abuse is the worst example of parents using open enrollment for their own, non-academic motives. Far more understandable are the relatively large numbers of commuting parents in Minnesota who have moved their children to schools closer to work or to day-care and latch-key programs.

Example. In Losing School District 4, over a hundred students left via open enrollment in the first two years of the program. Most were elementary students whose parents cited day-care or latch-key convenience as their reason for leaving. District 4 is located forty miles or so from a major metropolitan area, and many parents commute to urban jobs. The superintendent indicates that the board is now confronted with the dilemma of having to cut programs to absorb the losses in revenue, which are cumulative each year. At the same time, they have to consider adding day-care or latch-key programs to hold their student population. The frustration is that these new programs would have nothing to do with improving academic excellence, are not funded in any categorical way, and would further reduce the general fund resources available to maintain the current levels of academic programming.

The students left behind, in this case primarily secondary students, lose as their academic options are reduced to accommodate the convenience of commuting parents. But those left behind are not the only students who lose in this situation.

Example. The Smiths live in Losing District 4, and both parents commute to work in the metro area. Their only daughter, Karen, was in the fourth grade when open enrollment became available. Enrolling her in a suburban school thirty miles closer to work and right across the street from a latch-key program was much more convenient and consistent than relying on neighbors and daily rearrangements to provide after-school and dinner-hour supervision. Now when the parents want to work late or socialize with peers, Karen can stay at the latch-key program until 8:00 p.m. Karen was upset at having to leave her friends, especially her basketball buddies who had been playing "horse," "one-on-one," and "21" ever since they could pass a ball. They were really looking forward to playing as a team in the competitive elementary basketball program. When Karen's former team-mates were playing for the trophy by the end of the fifth grade, the Smiths could not understand why Karen did not want to go to the game.

Karen is a loser in this choice game, too. She lost her connection to her friends, her neighborhood, and her community. It would have been easier for Karen if her parents had simply moved closer to work. This hurt more because she still lived in one community, attended school in another, and participated in neither. The open enrollment plan is a social experiment of great magnitude, and many people have questioned the wisdom of introducing additional and heavy doses of change into the lives of young people. Adolescence is a time of life already overloaded with physical, social, emotional, and psychological changes. It is a period that seems to demand policies designed to provide security, stability, and continuity.

Sylvia Hewlett's book, *When the Bough Breaks*, is a disturbing examination of how children's needs have not been factored into policy equations. In summarizing a chapter, titled "Private Choices: Looking Out For Number One," she describes what she terms "twisting spiral of cumulative causation."

> Parents have become much more involved in looking out for Number One, and many of them have relinquished at least some responsibility for their children. . . . This abdication of authority has opened a window of opportunity for free enterprise. . . . Many of these goods and services are extremely convenient for parents—which is why they are so popular— but, by and large, they are destructive to children. Preoccupied parents, permissive laws and unregulated markets exacerbate one another and together create an environment that is remarkably antagonistic to young people. (Hewlett 1991: 133)

Hewlett suggests that instead of additional deregulation of services to children, government needs to act as guardian of America's children by passing new laws and regulations that would rein in unbridled parents and aggressive entrepreneurs. While her work does not discuss school choice directly, she does describe a kind of subtle synergism occurring among the variety of social policies affecting children that has significant destructive potential, a total effect far greater than the sum of these policies when examined independently. When choice is factored in, the synergistics will multiply exponentially. School choice is the most sweeping policy change ever proposed in terms of its effects on children. Children in general could be big losers in a choice market.

Proponents take as gospel the assumption that all parents are equally involved, concerned, and competent to make school choices. That is, at best, a naive assumption. It totally ignores the sociology of the inner city and fails to recognize that ineffective parenting plays a role in Peoria as well.

Example. Except for a few close friends, Bob had been an outsider throughout junior high school, socially inept, and never a part of the mainstream groups and cliques. When he fell in love with Mary and started dating in his sophomore year, his whole life changed. Mary open-enrolled to a neighboring school for her junior year, and Bob had to follow. His parents were concerned but unable or unwilling to control his decision. In fact, they gave him a car to drive to the new school. Mary broke up with him shortly after their transfer, having quickly made new friends and connections. Bob was never as good at making friends and was now rejected and alone in a new school. He became very depressed and skipped school frequently. His grades fell off sharply. He ended up in the psychiatric ward at the hospital by spring of his junior year. Bob's health improved; he took summer school to make up lost credits and returned to his resident high school for his senior year. He still has trouble talking about his "lost junior year."

How many parents will be like Bob's, too permissive, too preoccupied or too unassertive to exercise wise parenting when their children make sometimes casual or fickle choices out of vulnerability or in response to peer pressure? In contrast, what about parents who are too involved, too demanding?

Example. Paul was an excellent athlete, particularly in hockey. His parents had encouraged his involvement in hockey since he was five. His father had been a member of a championship team in high school and wanted the same or better for his son. The

parents belonged to the "blue-line" parents' organization, participated in all the fund-raisers to help pay for indoor ice, and had
gladly driven Paul to games and practices early in the morning,
late in the evening, and on weekends. Hockey was a part of life at
Paul's house. When he became starting goalie on the varsity team
his sophomore year, his parents were ecstatic. However, the team
did not have a winning season, and the decision was made to open
enroll in the neighboring high school—which did have a winning
team—for the junior season. There was a good chance for this team
to make the play-offs, for Paul to be scouted as a junior and get a
"free ride" to college. Paul transferred and made the starting
position. That's when the trouble started. Equally active hockey
parents and students in the new district were outraged that "outsiders" were being recruited and were taking the starting positions
away from their local players. Pressure was put on the coach, the
athletic director, even the school board. Paul was booed when
introduced at the start of a couple of home games.

Was Paul a winner or a loser? He did play in a lot more winning
games, but at what price? In Minnesota's unregulated public
school choice program, students can leave for any reason. Convenience, love, athletics are as good as any and the Karens, Bobs,
and Pauls who exercise the choice to leave can become the losers.
It isn't just those who stay behind who are hurt by choice.

Many who stay behind will do so because they are excluded
from choosing. If and when private schools are included in the mix
of choice programs, disabled students will be guaranteed few if
any choices. In 1991, a Wisconsin trial court, hearing a challenge
to the Milwaukee private school choice plan, found that

> Although participating schools could not discriminate on the
> basis of handicapping condition, neither did they have to
> make substantial adaptations to accommodate handicapped
> students or provide an appropriate education for handicapped
> students who wished to participate. (Underwood 1991: 18)

The new federal law, the Americans With Disabilities Act (ADA), includes provisions requiring compliance by private schools, which were not previously covered by the 1973 law, but it has loopholes: "Church-affiliated schools are exempt from compliance." "What the law does not do is require [private] schools to provide a special-education program or change admissions standards" (Vlader 1992: 18).

Choice programs, particularly those including private schools, exclude or discriminate against disabled students in two ways. First, there is no real choice if all participating schools are not required to provide the accommodations or additional services necessary to meet the needs of these students. Second, the proportion and concentration of the more costly, disabled students will increase in the public schools, which are required to serve all children. This means resources available for all students will be reduced. Once again, we will have implemented a public policy that tells disabled young people that they are disqualified from the opportunities available to others. These students will be a whole class of people in the losing column of the choice balance sheet.

The final entry on the losing side of the choice ledger is not an individual or even a class of individuals. It's the concept of community. In rural and small-town America, the public school is the focusing or centering institution of the community. The athletic events, music concerts, Christmas programs, school plays, prom grand marches, and graduation ceremonies bring all generations together regularly and traditionally. Community education and early childhood programs provide access and continuing participation from the youngest to the oldest. Gymnasiums, cooking and sewing labs, computer facilities, and shop equipment are used by students by day and by communities by night. Ownership is a key concept for the proponents of choice. Rural communities don't need choice to understand ownership of their schools. In fact, choice endangers their ownership.

In Minnesota, many small schools and districts that lost students in the first rounds of open enrollment are closing their doors. The numbers will only increase in the next few years. These costs of choice are much more difficult to quantify than the numbers suggest.

Example. Mrs. Nelson and Mrs. Thomas are heartbroken over the closing of their local K–12 school. They are part of a senior citizens group that was very active in the school. Their days always started at 7:00 a.m. with a brisk walk while their husbands gathered at the post office to discuss world affairs. In the winter, this walk took place up and down the long main hallway of the school. Members of their group served on the community education council and regularly took part in the programs. Mrs. Nelson was so proud that she had taken an introductory computer course and had made all the birthday cards for her grandchildren, who thought she was too old to learn new tricks. Mrs. Thomas taught a very popular cooking class every holiday season specializing in potica and other ethnic treats because she did not want the younger generations to lose their traditions. Beautiful and elaborate bird houses were Mr. Johnson's specialty, and he taught a woodworking class every winter quarter. He said he did it because he believed it was ecologically better to have birds eat the mosquitoes than to spray poisons. His wife said he did it to get out of the house and to put meaning into his life since retirement.

The school is closed now, and something important, and perhaps incalculable, has been lost. The community's kindergarten children get on a bus and travel twenty-five miles to the consolidated school. The kindergarten and elementary parents don't volunteer in the classroom like they used to. Distance, both geographic and social, is a barrier. They don't belong to an active—or inactive— PTA any more, and parent conferences are more impersonal and intimidating. Friday nights in the fall are strange without the football games, and everyone misses the band concerts. Even the Fourth of July, during summer vacation, brings melancholy memories of the marching bands that used to be. An entire community and all that means goes on the losing side of the ledger. Lake Wobegon will never be the same.

Of course, choice means winners and losers. The communities receiving the students through open enrollment and eventual consolidation are winners all around. The school districts receive hundreds of thousands of dollars each year with the new, open enrollment students. These additional dollars can be used to add more programs, which will attract new students each year and provide for the kinds of public relations programs that ensure that the good news travels. But receiving school districts are not the only beneficiary. It has been estimated that the economic benefit to the receiving communities is more than three times the value of the new school aid dollars. Understanding this, local businesses increase their sponsorship of school activities and promotions. Property values increase in the receiving communities as they decline in the losing communities.

Choice will result in more and more school closings and consolidations in rural America. Consolidation may mean more efficient use of education dollars in some cases, and "bigger is better" is always debatable.

> The data on consolidation remain inconclusive. Moreover, consolidating districts usually means closing some schools, and this has proved to be a serious matter, especially in small and rural school districts where the local school may be a focal point of the community's identity. (Ornstein 1990: 45)

Are all costs measured in dollars? Robert Cole writes: "Rural America and its schools must be healthy if the nation is to prosper . . . because these places are home, in a society where the idea of home is becoming an abstraction not rooted in a place" (Cole 1991: 110). Perhaps the importance of community should not be so casually disregarded in our policy debates about marketplace competition and choice in education.

Daly and Cobb make convincing arguments for re-evaluating the relationship between traditional economic theory and community: "But what is equally important for the new model—and absent in the traditional one—is the recognition that the well-being of a community as a whole is constitutive of each person's welfare" (Daly and Cobb 1989: 164). They quote Edward Schwarz:

It now appears certain that a strong, local community is essential to psychological well-being, personal growth, social order, and a sense of political efficacy. These conclusions are now emerging at the center of every social science discipline. (Daly and Cobb 1989: 17)

Most significantly, they argue: "Decisions that will be made soon in this country will shape the world of our children and grand-children, probably irreversibly. They should not be made within the restricted context that now governs the academic discipline of economics" (Daly and Cobb 1989: 19).

Choice is traditional economics applied to education, and the marketplace competition produces winners and losers. When the losing column on the choice balance sheet is added up, the costs may be too high. Hubert Humphrey once said, "The moral test of government is how it treats those who are in the dawn of life, the children; those who are in the twilight of life, the aged; and those who are in the shadows of life—the sick, the needy and the handicapped."

On this test, choice is morally bankrupt.

10

Choice and the Professionals

According to former Governor Perpich, choice has opened up "more exciting opportunities for teachers" (Nathan 1989b: 3). Nathan suggests that choice has helped "raise morale of educators who were allowed to create distinctive programs from which families select" (Nathan 1989b: 203). Raywid says,

> Schools of choice are able to minimize, if not eliminate, major sources of teacher dissatisfaction. These have been identified as powerlessness, professional isolation, the extreme frag- mentation of the work day and the educational task, the depersonalized circumstances of large schools, the low es- teem in which teachers are held, severe discipline problems, and external mandates which interfere with effective teaching and productive interaction with students. (Raywid 1989: 19)

Sound too good to be true? It certainly is for many teachers in Minnesota. Recall that Minnesota's choice program is inter-district, not intra-district, and the state aids travel across district lines. This is a critical difference.

Example. In Losing District 5, the summer and fall of 1989 was a nightmare for educators. The controversial closing of one of the district's two high schools coincided with the first year of open enrollment. Over 50 percent of the district's 550 secondary students filed the transfer forms for the 1989–90 school year. As a result, the school board reversed its decision to close the school and the waiting game began. How many students would return? Preparing for the worst, administrators had placed 30 percent of the teachers on unrequested leave of absence (ULA) in the spring, as required by legal timelines. Administrators had also constructed two master schedules for the high school: one to use if none of the open enrollment students showed up the first day and one to use if most returned. District administrators worked as closely as possible with the surrounding receiving districts to nail down numbers, but nobody knew anything for certain. Administrators scratched their heads, the least senior teachers waited it out on ULA, and 25-year, senior teachers watched their teaching assignments change from day to day as recall realignments shifted with shifting enrollment numbers.

Low morale, feelings of powerlessness and isolation were all affected by choice, but not for the better. The feelings of isolation only increased a year later, when one of the neighboring, "winning" school districts negotiated a 1991–93 salary bonus for its teachers if enrollment increased over the previous year. Teachers in another of Losing District 5's neighboring districts became concerned about the possible dissolution of District 5 and wrote letters to their legislators seeking protection for their jobs. No teacher involved would call these "exciting opportunities." Similar situations have occurred in several Minnesota communities since 1989, and nothing but chance and coincidence determines which district and which educators will get it next. The administrators were stressed, but the teachers were unemployed. The students and state aids found a home, but teacher's rights did not follow.

This is particularly demoralizing for teachers in Minnesota because every other law concerning school district reorganization provides some employment protection. In the 1991 Education Laws of Minnesota, at least six statutes (122.242, 122.245, 122.532, 122.541, 122.937, 122.95) require school districts reorganizing, cooperating, combining, dissolving, or forming education districts to employ teachers based on a combined seniority list. Even statute MS. 122.535 provides for severance pay for teachers laid off as a result of an "Agreement for Secondary Education" (Minnesota Education Laws 1991, vol. 1, pp. 176–215). Is it any wonder that teachers laid off as a result of open enrollment, especially for reasons totally unrelated to expanded student academic opportunity, feel isolated, powerless, and forgotten? Perhaps Raywid's low esteem was better than no esteem, which is what teachers got under Minnesota's inter-district open enrollment?

Is there hope for these teachers laid off or facing layoffs in these losing districts? Will the neighboring districts become the white knights of the education marketplace and bail out the losing school districts with consolidation, cooperation and combination, dissolution and attachment? Probably not. Why should they, when these arrangements include obligations not only for teacher seniority, but for the assumption of long-term indebtedness and all facility maintenance? The only incentive in open enrollment is to accept the new students and reap the windfall profits—all with no strings attached. It's a whole new way of doing education business in Minnesota.

Granted, some of the teachers laid off from Losing District 5 were employed in the receiving districts. But this was not done according to seniority, and it usually required these teachers to take a substantial cut in pay and to accept new seniority dates, sometimes after ten to fifteen years of experience. These were the winners who got a job? Union leaders and activists need not apply, of course.

Teachers in the smallest districts are the most vulnerable. Shifting enrollments, blowing in the winds of day-care convenience, local elections, or political controversy will result in unpredictable pockets of teacher unemployment. These teachers have none of the seniority protections included in other legislation. In many cases, they won't be employed in the receiving districts because their experience and advanced degrees are too expensive. Why should they be hired, when the receiving districts can hire two teachers right out of college for the price of one laid-off veteran? One has to wonder whether this failure to address teacher seniority in the open enrollment legislation was a mere oversight.

However, the advocates of school choice would have us believe that the teachers involved love it. Raywid quotes a teacher: "Alternative education stimulates personal and academic growth of staff as much as students." She cites the Philadelphia example: "After a year, 38 of the 39 involuntarily shifted teachers chose the alternative school in preference to any other assignment" (Raywid 1989: 19–22).

Nathan describes his experience at the St. Paul Open School: "Teachers were allowed to combine classroom learning with community service; we were able to use the whole continent as a place to learn, often taking cross-country trips as the final activity in a class" (Nathan 1989b: 11).

Let's be very clear here. All of the discussions and examples that describe how good choice is for teachers refer to intra-district, not inter-district choice—alternatives and choices within a single jurisdiction. There is absolutely no quarrel with the concept that all students and all teachers do not learn and teach most effectively in the same way. Having taught secondary social studies for four years at the Duluth Open School, I know the personal and professional benefits of alternative education, and I saw it in my students. The critical difference is that only my teaching assignment changed with changing enrollment, not my teaching career! That's why I was free to try new material and explore new methods.

Even Charles Glenn, a cautious advocate for public school choice, wrote:

> Any choice policy we might develop that ignores the rights and legitimate interests of teachers will not work to strengthen public education, though it may satisfy a few parents at the expense of many children. Teachers who are treated unfairly or who fear that parent choice will undermine their position are not going to take the lead in making schools more diverse, more flavorful, more effective. (Glenn 1989: 157)

Perhaps it will be the new outcome-based charter schools to the rescue for unemployed teachers in Minnesota. Although designed to create innovative, outcome-based schools, one of the first charters granted was for a bail-out. The Toivola-Meadowlands school, one of six K–12 schools in a large, sparsely populated, consolidated school district in northern Minnesota, has been closed by the district's board of education for the 1993–94 school year. The school had lost over 30 percent of its students since open enrollment began and was costing close to $5,000 per pupil to operate. In January 1992, the Minnesota State Board of Education approved a proposal to turn it into a charter school for the 1993–94 school year, the only K–12 charter granted. The vote was close, 5–4, with many state board members concerned about the substantial loss of revenue the charter school will face. While the new school will receive state aid per pupil, it cannot levy to increase resources and will not benefit from the existing levies of the larger district.

What looks on the surface like an opportunity for the teachers laid off by the school closing may not be what it seems. Teachers have to be granted leaves of absence to teach in the new charter schools, but they have to pay both the employer and employee parts of the pension contribution to maintain their retirement benefits. These contributions will be calculated on their previous salaries, not their charter salaries. Because the new charter school will have to operate with close to $2,000 less per pupil, the new salaries will probably be much lower than those paid by the established public school district. These are the "new professional opportunities for teachers" the law was established to create.

In addition, the legislation states: "Except as provided in this section, an outcome-based school is exempt from all statutes and rules applicable to a school board or school district" (MS 120.064, subd. 7). There is no mention in the provisions of seniority, continuing contract, tenure or any other system of determining which teachers are hired, fired, laid off, or recalled. "The board may discharge teachers and nonlicensed employees" is all there is (MS 120.064, subd. 11). All protections are eliminated for teachers in charter schools, as advocated by the proponents of choice.

Seniority and tenure are favorite targets and scapegoats in the current wave of school-bashing. For Chubb and Moe, they are part of the deadening bureaucracy of administrative constraints that make public schools ineffective. "Professionalism and tenure are antithetical," says Chester Finn, Jr., a former Assistant Secretary of Education and a proponent of free-market solutions to educational problems (Allis 1991: 64).

Governor Weld of Massachusetts "wants to allow school principals free rein to make hiring and firing decisions without reference to tenure or job security. 'This isn't anti-teacher,' says Weld. 'It's anti-slob teacher' " (Allis 1991: 64). How's that for a healthy dose of low esteem?

In Chubb and Moe's new marketplace system of educational choice, "statewide tenure laws will be eliminated" (Chubb and Moe 1990: 223). "Teachers will continue to have a right to join unions and engage in collective bargaining" (p. 224). Anyone who has ever worked anywhere close to the front lines in education knows that combination is both naive and contradictory. Chubb and Moe even contradict themselves.

> Precisely because the principal is able to build a hand-picked team of "right-thinking" teachers whom he respects and trusts, teachers are not a threat to his leadership. . . . Teachers who are team players . . . are hardly good candidates for union membership. (Chubb and Moe 1990: 52–53)

Before this disintegrates into as simplistic a defense of seniority and tenure as is the rhetoric of their detractors, let's attempt a more realistic analysis. The theory behind tenure and seniority is sound and rational: "Tenure is a creation of statute designed to maintain adequate, permanent and qualified teaching staffs free from political and personal arbitrary interference" (*Deskbook* 1985: 379). The courts have agreed with this purpose of tenure

> to promote good order and the welfare of the school system by preventing removal of capable and experienced teachers

at the personal whims of changing office holders; to protect and improve state education by retaining in their positions teachers who are qualified and capable and who have demonstrated their fitness; and to prevent the dismissal of such teachers without just cause. (*Deskbook* 1985: 380)

The sound theory is less than perfect in practice. The process for removing an incompetent teacher has become long and expensive due, in part, to the number of hearings and appeals required. In twenty-three years in education as school board member, district and building administrator, and teacher, I have known all the frustrations of working with, supervising, and terminating incompetent teachers. But I also know that the knee-jerk response to these frustrations of simply eliminating tenure and seniority, without understanding and replacing their theoretical function, is very dangerous.

Example. Mr. Jones is a fifteen-year veteran teacher. He is loved by his fifth-grade students and held in high esteem by parents and peers. When the district administration imposed—without discussion or consultation with the teachers—a new, tracked reading program on the school, he was concerned. The teachers arrived on the first day of school that fall to find that all the old texts and materials had been confiscated and the new system was in place. At the opening in-service meeting, it was explained that the reading periods had been extended, and each classroom had to have four reading groups, as determined by ability. Teachers were told they had to follow the instructor's manuals word for word, page by page. Mr. Jones questioned whether the students were actually getting more reading time, since the longer block of instructional time had to be divided among the four groups. He also questioned the wisdom of identifying some students as slower than others, worried about self-concept and incentive to learn. Mr. Jones's questions were not welcome by the principal; they were taken as a challenge to his authority. As a result, Mr. Jones had two full school days of "supervisory evaluation," including noon hours. The resulting write-up was very negative, personally and professionally. Without the protection of tenure, Mr. Jones would have been history.

Example. Ms. Smith was a ten-year veteran teacher, competent in the classroom beyond doubt, who had been elected local union president by her peers. She was also active in the union organization at the regional and state levels. As local president, she served as grievance chairperson for the district. Her efforts in holding the district to the terms of the master agreement, including the issue of the employment of non-licensed personnel in teacher assignments, resulted in favorable arbitration decisions and earned her the animosity of the board and administration. For three consecutive years, her classroom assignment was changed. While the right-of-assignment was clearly administrative prerogative, everyone knew it was pay-back time. Without the protection of tenure, Ms. Smith would have joined Mr. Jones in the annals of history.

Tenure protects many precious commodities—academic freedom, freedom of speech and association, the right to bargain collectively—in addition to the theoretical purposes cited in statutes and court decisions. Tenure provides the protective environment that encourages the kinds of energetic, creative, and innovative teaching called for in the deregulatory rhetoric of choice. Believe it or not, there are a lot of administrators out there who do not welcome change and "boat-rocking."

But tenure also affords a significant degree of protection for incompetent teachers. Certainly the processes and procedures that have evolved around teacher termination are to blame, but only in part. A substantial part of the problem rests squarely on the shoulders of unassertive, insecure, incompetent, poorly trained and/or complacent administrators. It is ironic that little or none of the rhetoric on choice and deregulation, with the obligatory elimination of teacher tenure and seniority, addresses this issue. The termination of an incompetent teacher requires time, emotional balance, training in the laws, attention to detail, documentation of incompetence, and the willingness to take action. It also requires just cause. Most of the onerous, procedural obstacles have been constructed because the administrative skills or the just cause were lacking. Abuse is the engine that drives regulation.

The problems of teacher termination are analogous to the problems of law enforcement. Just as the courts were forced to interpret the rights of the accused to ensure equal protection and due process, so have the substantive and procedural safeguards been increased surrounding teacher terminations. Just as the police have had to learn to do it right and for the right reasons, so administrators have to learn to do it for the right reasons and in the right way. It's a myth that it is impossible to fire an incompetent teacher. The myth has been carefully constructed to camouflage administrative incompetence.

It is truly amazing that so little in all the hype about the crisis and need for reform, restructuring, deregulating, considers the possibility that administrative incompetence might just be a major part of the problem. It's been my experience, having employed, supervised, and worked with and for many administrators, that the ratio of competence to incompetence is no better in the administrative profession than in the teaching profession. The big difference is the degree of influence any administrative incompetence has: One incompetent teacher may affect 30 elementary students or 150 secondary students. One incompetent building administrator may directly affect ten to fifty or more teachers and, indirectly, all the students in a school.

This argument was solidly supported, if in reverse order, by the effective schools research of the early 1980s. Although the assumptions and methodology of the total body of effective schools research have been questioned, the studies consistently found that strong administrative leadership made a key difference in effective schools. Common sense suggests that administrative incompetence also makes a difference. That it exists should come as no surprise; that it is routinely ignored is surprising and frustrating.

It is an inside joke in the profession that incompetent administrators were once teachers who couldn't cut it in the classroom, so they went into administration. After all, the training and licensing are less rigorous for administrators than for the initial teaching degree, and often involve just writing papers and accumulating seat-time in extension-type programs that are not a part of any graduate school. These programs do not have the admission standards of a graduate school and do not include anything as practical as student teaching. Worse yet, an FBI investigation, Operation Dipscam (short for diploma scam) revealed that education was one of the most common fields for which bogus degrees were purchased from diploma mills (Wolcott 1990: 71).

Example. Dr. James was hired very quickly by a district whose superintendent had left to take a new position. After two years on the job, Dr. James was embarrassed by a local newspaper story documenting the fact that he had forged several letters of recommendation he had used to secure a previous position. He withheld his current application file from the press on the advice of his attorney. Further investigation revealed that he had received his doctorate from a "non-traditional," "non-residential" university out of state. The advertisement for that university offered "economical home-study for Bachelor's, Master's, Ph.D., with credits for independent study and life-experience."

It is never mentioned in the attacks on teacher tenure that excellent teachers might require protection from incompetent, arbitrary, or capricious administrators. It is also of significance that administrators (except superintendents) in Minnesota and most states have the same continuing contract (tenure and seniority) and collective bargaining protections that teachers enjoy. It can be argued from the Dr. James example that superintendents don't need the protection of tenure, because they usually work for lay boards that do not always have the skills or training to properly screen candidates or document for termination. Principals have the same protection, a similar ratio of incompetence with much broader impact, but nowhere near the negative press in the current rhetoric of crisis and choice. But ask any superintendent or board how far they can get with any change or reform without competent and enthusiastic principals. Of course, there aren't as many of them in terms of numbers and dollars, and breaking the back of administrative tenure will not have anywhere near the same yield in terms of cost reduction and "load-shedding" as will breaking the back of teacher tenure.

Even the most competent administrators will have their tasks complicated and multiplied by enrollment choice. In Minnesota, open enrollment is an administrative conundrum. Administrators in districts that students leave will be busy cutting programs to make up for lost enrollment, just when they should be adding programs to attract new enrollment and revenue. The most routine tasks can be fraught with the danger of lost students. The elementary principal has to think twice before dividing 81 second-grade students into 3 sections of 27 rather than 4 sections of 20 when the neighboring district advertises small elementary class size. The high school principal has to be very careful in cutting electives with low registrations if those students closed out or conflicted pick up and leave. How about the athletic director's recommendation to drop a varsity sport? The only peg to hang an administrative hat on was the deadlines for open enrollment applications. At least there was a point in time after which some degree of planning was possible. However, several exceptions to the deadlines have been added and a spokesperson for the state department of education was quoted in February 1991 as stating that the deadlines would eventually be dropped.

If there are soft deadlines or no deadlines, the tasks of budgeting, staffing, and scheduling become even more difficult. Parents and students can decide at any time—as they can regarding the charter schools—or change their minds at any time. This is not to suggest that parents and/or students might be fickle, but what if they are? What if eleventh-hour political compromise is reached in a home district and significant numbers of students choose not to leave? The non-resident administrators will already have scheduled space and hired staff to make room for these students, while the home district will have laid off teachers and closed course sections. Open enrollment makes administrative planning the oxymoron of education.

Public relations becomes a critical component of the administrative job. Perhaps it always was to some degree, but the stakes just went sky high. Believing that advertising for students is unprofessional, or that competing for students is illegal (MS 123.35, subd. 14: "school districts shall not compete with one another for the enrollment of students") won't help if the neighboring district is putting flyers in McDonald's lunch bags. When are the stakes high enough to compromise integrity, to fudge the facts a little, massage the test scores a little, to create a better image? When does the Machiavellian ethic of ends justifying means become the order of the day?

When busy administrators are engaged in public relations work, what isn't getting done? Attention to discipline, attendance, staff development, curriculum revision, building maintenance, efficient transportation routing, teacher evaluations and conferences, classroom observations, reports for the school board, policy review and recommendation, scheduling, reading for professional growth, preparation for faculty inservice, investigation of child abuse? The list is endless and most administrators will say, without hesitation, that there is never enough time.

If the state of the art now includes teachers' contracts with enrollment bonuses, what happens to administrative priorities when enrollment numbers become a part of their performance evaluation? When dropping enrollment threatens their salary increases or job security? Imagine the frustration when administrators are held responsible for enrollment factors over which they have no control, such as a distant school board decision, or for athletics, or day-care convenience or to escape high graduation requirements.

Example. In 1985, Losing School District 6 accepted the recommendation of the high school faculty senate, working with the administration, parents and board members, to increase the total graduation requirements from fifteen credits in grades ten to twelve to eighteen credits, one of which had to be in science and one of which had to be in mathematics. The previous requirements had minimally complied with the state's and did not include any science or math at the high school level. The required courses for graduation would now include three years of English, three years of social studies, one year of science, one year of math, one-half year of health and one-half year of physical education. Nine courses would be required; the balance of nine credits needed to meet the eighteen credit requirement would consist of elective choice. The high school schedule provided a seven-period day, so it was still possible for students to carry six courses per year and have a study hall. The changes were phased in over three years, with the class of 1989 being the first to graduate under the new credit requirement. Losing District 6 had more than a thousand students and was included in the first mandatory year of open enrollment. Several students had the system figured out. They transferred for the fall of 1989–90 to neighboring districts that still operated under the state minimums. With a six-period day, they were out and on the job an hour earlier each day.

In Minnesota, choice came in but most regulation stayed. The results do not empower teachers and administrators or weed out the incompetent. It's like competing in a race with your laces tied together. The point is obviously not to attack the regulations and legal constraints, most of which are essential to protect the institution of public education in a democratic society. The point is that unrestricted, interdistrict, public school choice, which is gaining momentum nationwide, is much more than meets the eye. For professionals, it can be like playing Russian roulette, never knowing when or why it's your turn to lose—students, revenues, jobs.

11

Choice and the Constitutions

The Fourteenth Amendment to the U.S. Constitution states:

No State shall make or enforce any law which shall abridge the privileges or immunities of citizens of the United States; nor shall any State deprive any person of life, liberty, or property, without due process of law, nor deny to any person within its jurisdiction the equal protection of the laws.

Choice will benefit some schools (and some students) at the expense of others. Proponents don't disagree; in fact, that's the purpose. "Choice works, and it works with a vengeance," said Reagan. To even an untrained legal observer, that premise seems to conflict with the Fourteenth Amendment. If an equitable education is not an expressed right in the Constitution, isn't it at least a privilege of all citizens? Shouldn't all citizens in a democracy be equally immune from the deprivations of ignorance? If education is commonly acknowledged as necessary to acquire property, don't all citizens have a property right to an equitable education? If a person is too poor to own property but still pays sales taxes that support education and votes in school elections, doesn't that qualify as citizenship and ownership and constitute a property right deserving of equal protection? Doesn't equal protection mean equal benefit when public money is raised by public officials to provide a public good?

How do all citizens exercise their First Amendment freedoms of speech and press if some citizens can choose a better education than others and if their choices diminish the educational opportunities of others? Isn't the expressed power of the federal government to provide for the general welfare sufficient to imply that some responsibility for the equitable education of all its citizens (upon which its very existence depends) is necessary and proper? Doesn't reading Jefferson and Madison remove any doubt about their original intent?

Perhaps this is nothing but the naive ramblings of an untrained legal mind. After all, the Supreme Court found in the 1973 Rodriguez case that education was not a "fundamental right" under the U.S. Constitution and was not subject to the Equal Protection guarantees. However, the vote was close, 5 to 4. Furthermore, had the case been heard by the Warren Court, the decision might have been different. When choice is factored into the education equation and the inequity balance tips even further, the Supreme Court will undoubtedly have another opportunity to determine whether glaring disparities and absolute deprivation have any equal protection remedy.

In the meantime, education-equity litigation proceeds in over half the states. Almost all state constitutions have specific education clauses that provide for thorough, general, efficient, free, equitable and/or uniform systems of public schools. It does seem ironic that school children are taught to pledge allegiance to the American flag, but it is left to state courts to protect the equality of the classrooms they are taught in. In December 1991, Minnesota District Judge Gary Meyer ruled that parts of the state's school finance system violate the state constitution and result in a "significant imbalance and inequity" between wealthy and poor school districts. He stated that the original goals of the 1971 "Minnesota miracle," which increased the proportion of foundation aid and restricted the use of property taxes had been severely eroded (*Saint Paul Pioneer Press* 1991: 21A).

Minnesota's education clause reads: "The stability of a republican form of government depending mainly upon the intelligence of the people, it is the duty of the Legislature to establish a general and uniform system of public schools." Judge Meyer also recognized in his decision the emphasis on education in a democratic government and "education's critical importance in supporting the viability of other civil liberties contained in the Bill of Rights." He stated that the mandate of uniformity is not diminished because the legislature has delegated much of its financing authority to local school districts. The rule of uniformity is ultimately the legislature's concern.

If the legislature's responsibility for a general and uniform system of public schools cannot be relegated to local control, how can it be left to individual choice? Any choice system that allows state aid (tuitions, scholarships, vouchers) to follow the students decreases the resources left to educate those who stay behind, many of whom have no effective choice. "General and uniform" become the myths of choice. School districts losing "choice" state revenue are forced into even greater reliance on the inequitable local property tax. The arguments for local control and continued property tax funding, for the right of each school district to address the educational needs of its children in any manner it sees fit, sound as American as the right of parents to choose their children's schools. The rhetoric is American; the consequences are not. That reasoning gave us legal segregation before *Brown vs. Board of Education*, gross inequities before New Jersey (1973), Kentucky (1989), Texas (1989), and so on. Choice will ultimately set off a whole new round of equity litigation.

If the choice systems adopted include public funding for parochial schools, the court challenges will not be limited to equity and equal protection issues. Chubb and Moe (1990: 219) advocate such a system: "Our own preference would be to include religious schools as well, as long as their sectarian functions can be kept clearly separate from their educational functions." The initiative filed in California for the November 1992 election would enable parents to send their children to parochial schools at taxpayers' expense, with assurances that those schools would remain free from "onerous regulation" (Olson 1991c: 18). The Pennsylvania Senate has approved a plan that would allow parents to use state stipends to sent their children to any public, private, or religious school (Viadero 1991: 17). In 1991–92, the Bush administration lobbied hard for a multimillion-dollar choice program that included religious schools (Miller 1992: 1). Public money for religious education is on deck, and lawyers will benefit from the largest job creation program of the century.

The polls show that a majority of Americans favor school choice. Short-sighted politicians will undoubtedly continue to enact choice legislation, and the courts will be busier than ever. So be it. The courts' role has always been that of a last resort for the

> rights of "politically impotent minorities." By definition, the processes of democracy bode poorly for the security of such rights. Thus, the task of guarding these constitutionally prescribed liberties sensibly falls upon a body that is not politically responsible, that is not beholden to the grace of the excited majoritarianism—the United States Supreme Court. Herein lies the great justification for the power of judicial review, the wisdom of Marbury v. Madison. (Lockhart, Kamisar, and Choper 1970: 23)

The courts have already wrestled for decades over the wall of separation between church and state erected by the establishment clause of the First Amendment. How high is the wall when considering public aid to parochial schools? The current, excessive entanglement standard was first applied by the Supreme Court in *Lemon v. Kurtzman* (1971).

> To be constitutional, a State's school aid law must meet these requirements: (1) the purpose of the aid must be clearly secular, not religious, (2) its primary effect must neither

advance nor inhibit religion, and (3) it must avoid an "excessive entanglement of government with religion." (McClenaghan 1990: 108)

Clearly, the choice programs being proposed will fail to meet these standards. Who will determine how much of the general state aid is spent for secular rather than religious purposes? The government will, and that's got to be excessive entanglement.

Many state constitutions, like Minnesota's, include explicit prohibitions of public aid for religious schools. Article XIII, Section 2, states: "In no case shall any public money or property be appropriated or used for the support of schools wherein the distinctive doctrines, creeds or tenets of any particular Christian or other religious sect are promulgated or taught" (*Legislative Manual* 1991–92: 46). In addition, the taxing authority provided in the Minnesota constitution states that taxes can be levied and collected for public purposes only. The Minnesota Bill of Rights is more specific than the federal version and states in Section 16: "Nor shall any man be compelled to attend, erect or support any place of worship, or to maintain any religious or ecclesiastical ministry, against his consent" (*Legislative Manual* 1991–92: 35).

There are several concerns, besides the federal and state constitutional issues cited above, about providing public funding for private and parochial schools through a choice system. It is generally accepted that public schools play an important democratizing role in bringing students of different religious, ethnic, and cultural backgrounds together. The draining of resources from the public schools to support private and parochial schools can only erode that primary mission. Choice will further facilitate the separation of children in schools and the reasons for that separation, religious or secular, are most often tied to ethnic, social, racial, or economic differences. It's race and/or class all over again.

Combine private and parochial school choice with deregulatory zeal, and any semblance of fair competition disappears. If public schools are going to be forced to compete with taxpayer-subsidized private schools, do we require compliance with the rules for all players, or do we drop the rules equally for all players? "In most cases, the proponents of private-school choice want it both ways. They want government money on the one hand but freedom from government regulation on the other" (Weinberg 1992: 40). If we drop the regulations across the board, do we take the time to examine the reasons for the regulations in the first place? What abuses do we reopen the doors to, and what protections do we eliminate? If regulatory compliance is only required of public schools, then why not scratch Jefferson and simply proceed with a much more deliberate, efficient, and humane dismantling of the public school system?

More likely, choice funding for private and parochial schools will turn out to be a mixed blessing for them in the long run. Government funding means government strings, eventually and inevitably, if not initially.

> If experience elsewhere is any indicator, accountability measures will accompany any substantial flow of money to private schools. The resulting intrusion on the autonomy and independence of the private sector threatens its uniqueness as an alternative to public schools. The publicization of private schools serves neither the schools, their clients, nor American education in general. (Kemerer 1992: 42)

While the role of private and parochial schools is not the same as that of public schools in our society, it is no less important. The importance of that role is totally dependent upon the freedom from government involvement or entanglement. Freedom of choice may become a myth for private and parochial schools once they accept government funding, and another thread in the traditional fabric of our democratic society will be torn apart by choice.

The ultimate paradox of choice is that it will inevitably eliminate choices—not for the few, but for the many. There will be fewer schools in rural America and fewer resources and options in the inner city. It's a policy designed to skim the best and write off the rest in the ghettos and a policy that will destroy community and tradition in much of America. As Lewis Finch, former superintendent of the Anoka-Hennepin school district, wrote about Minnesota's open enrollment: "Ultimately, the state will have islands of education excellence surrounded by vast wastelands of deprivation." When schools asked for help, they got choice—"the great placebo" (Finch 1989: 13).

One business with a vested interest in reading agrees that choice is not the answer. On the September 27, 1991, cover, *Publisher's Weekly* urged President Bush to read Kozol's *Savage Inequalities*:

It is the story of how, in our public schools, we are creating a country profoundly different from the one our founders envisaged. It is the story of two nations that are separate and unequal in their educational facilities, and tells how this unfair imbalance has been created and maintained by the inequitable distribution of public funds. Clearly, something must be done about American education, but too often those who work to reform it do so through notions of "choice" and "competition," market terms that have no place in a debate on the needs of our poor children. In the end, there is no doubt that we will have to spend money, and a lot of it, to bring genuine equality to our schools.

But President Bush cautioned parents of poor children that money was not a cure for education problems, that "a society that worships money . . . is a society in peril" (Kozol 1991: 205). Cold and callous words for parents who only want a fair chance for their kids. Senator Orrin Hatch (R-Utah) said, while pushing Bush's choice program in Congress, "Let's give the low-income parents at least one additional weapon for use for school improvement. Let's give them the ability to walk out" (Miller 1992b: 26). Hatch is right on: Choice is the very least they could give.

Jefferson warned that education would cost. But he also warned that the cost is not more than the "thousandth part" of what will be paid if the people are left in ignorance. We can pay now or pay a lot more later. What if choice sweeps the land and the "failing" public schools are replaced by private "scholarship" schools? What if the new schools turn out to be elitist, separatist, or just plain terrible? What if it becomes necessary to reconstruct rural school districts where there are no schools or communities left, to rebuild urban public schools to bring all poor people into the mainstream of American life?

> At that point it would be incredibly difficult to persuade the middle class to support a substantial new program that would help only people who don't pay taxes. Before taking such an immense risk, we ought to make sure we've tried every possible means of making bad schools better which doesn't involve cutting them loose from the webbing of public life. (Lemann 1991: 105)

Making sure we've tried every possible alternative means more money and emphasis on research. However, the research must be independent and objective, not vulnerable to political pressure or subject to political suppression. This is already a part of the partisan battle over education in Washington with the reauthorization of the Education Department's office of educational research and improvement. "The lightning rod is a proposal to create an independent body to oversee its operations—and prevent the Administration from using the agency to further its political agenda, a longtime concern on Capitol Hill" (Miller 1992a: 21).

We need more information and answers before we launch this massive social experiment. But the information has to be good; the risks are too great, the potential costs too high to settle for anything less.

What if the only cost of choice is not in future repair bills? If Polly Williams takes her children out of the Milwaukee public schools, but her neighborhood erupts as a result of increasing impoverishment and ignorance, what has she gained? (Shapiro 1991: 58).

Recall that Jefferson also warned: "Educate and inform the

whole mass of the people. Enable them to see that it is their interest to preserve peace and order, and they will preserve them." It is absolutely fundamental to a democratic society that each individual's rights and freedoms are inescapably dependent on everyone else's. As Martin Luther King Jr. wrote from the Birmingham jail, "Injustice anywhere is a threat to justice everywhere" (McClenaghan 1990: 159).

My goal in this work has been to raise questions, to urge caution and further study before risking choice as a panacea for the problems in American education. My fear is that the work will be discounted either as the self-serving interests of a "professional" or presumptuous ideas of a mere classroom teacher. My commitment is that the choice bandwagon will not have rolled over the land without challenge—not on my watch. My hope is that our grandchildren will still have choices and not be burdened by our mistakes.

References

Albertson, Gary D. September 12, 1991a. "ISD 710 Board Approves Teacher's Contract." *Cook News-Herald.*

————. October 31, 1991b. "T-M Closing Process Started." *Cook News-Herald.*

————. November 14, 1991c. "They're Taking Our Children . . . And The State Says It's OK." *Cook News-Herald.*

Allis, Sam. December 23, 1991. "Laying Siege to Seniority." *Time.*

Bastian, Ann. February 1990. "Thoughts on School Choice." *The Education Digest.*

Becker, Gary S. December 18, 1989. "What Our Schools Need Is a Healthy Dose Of Competition." *Business Week.*

Bergstrom, Howard. 1990. *Report on a Study of Minnesota Community College Involvement in the Postsecondary Enrollment Options Program.* Unpublished manuscript for the Minnesota Community College System.

Bloomquist, Lee. December 8, 1991. "Open Enrollment Helping Larger Range Schools." *Hibbing Daily Tribune.*

Bracey, Gerald W. October 1991. "Why Can't They Be Like We Were?" *Phi Delta Kappan.*

Brandl, John. 1989. "An Education Policy Agenda for Legislators." In *Public Schools by Choice,* edited by Joe Nathan. St. Paul, Minn.: Institute for Learning and Teaching.

Bridge, R. G., and J. Blackman. 1978. "Family Choice in American

Education." *A Study of Alternatives in American Education* (vol. 4). Santa Monica, Calif.: The Rand Corporation.

Castro, Janice, and Richard Woodbury. October 28, 1991. "The Man Who Fired a Dog to Save a Buck." *Time.*

Chubb, John E., and Terry M. Moe. 1990. *Politics, Markets, and America's Schools.* Washington, D.C.: Brookings Institution.

———. February 20, 1991. "A Response to Our Critics." *Education Week.*

Clark, J. R., and Michael Veseth. 1987. *Economics: Cost and Choice.* New York: Harcourt Brace Jovanovich.

Cole, Robert. April 1991. "Ghosts in Small-Town Schools." *The Education Digest.*

Daly, Herman E., and John B. Cobb, Jr. 1989. *For the Common Good.* Boston: Beacon Press.

Darling-Hammond, Linda. November 1991. "The Implications of Testing Policy for Quality and Equality." *Phi Delta Kappan.*

Deskbook of Encyclopedia of American School Law. 1985. Rosemount, Minn.: Data Research, Inc.

Diegmueller, Karen. May 13, 1992. "Mass. Education Panel Votes to Repeal Choice Law." *Education Week.*

Education Week. June 3, 1992. "Across the Nation: States."

Education Week. January 8, 1991. "Minn. Judge Rules Against School Finance System."

Elam, Stanley M. September 1990. "The 22nd Annual Gallup Poll of the Public's Attitudes Toward the Public Schools." *Phi Delta Kappan.*

Elam, Stanley M., Lowell C. Ross, and Alec M. Gallup. September 1991. "The 23rd Annual Gallup Poll of the Public's Awareness Toward the Public Schools." *Phi Delta Kappan.*

Elmore, R. F. 1986. *Choice in Public Education.* Report No. JNE-01. Santa Monica, Calif.: The Rand Corporation.

———. 1988. "Choice in Public Education." In *The Politics of Excellence and Choice in Education,* edited by W. L. Boy and C. T. Kerchner. New York: Falmer.

Fierman, Jaclyn. December 4, 1989. "Giving Parents A Choice of Schools." *Fortune.*

Finch, Lewis W. November 1989. "Choice: Claims of Success, Predictions of Failure." *The Education Digest.*

First, Patricia F. 1991. "The Policy Questions Surrounding the Financing of Choice." In *Financing School Choice*. Oak Brook, Ill.: North Central Regional Educational Laboratory.

Glenn, Charles. 1989. "Putting Choice in Place." In *Public Schools by Choice*, edited by Joe Nathan. St. Paul, Minn.: Institute for Learning and Teaching.

Goodgame, Dan. November 25, 1991. "Why Bigotry Still Works at Election Time." *Time*.

Heath, A. 1976. *Rational Choice and Social Exchange*. Cambridge, England: Cambridge University Press.

Helmberger, Marshall. November 18, 1991. "Future of T/M School in Hands of Residents." *The Timberjay*.

Hewlett, Sylvia Ann. 1991. *When the Bough Breaks: The Cost of Neglecting Our Children*. New York: Basic Books.

Hotakainen, Rob. September 9, 1990. "Busing Battle." *Minneapolis Star Tribune*.

Jefferson, Thomas. 1939. *Democracy*. Edited by Saul K. Padover. New York: D. Appleton-Century.

Johnson, Haynes. 1991. *Sleepwalking Through History*. New York: W. W. Norton.

Kemerer, Frank R. January 8, 1992. "The Publicization of the Private School." *Education Week*.

Kennedy, Tony. January 31, 1989. "Minnesota's Schools' Open Enrollment Gets Mixed Reviews." *St. Petersburg Times*.

Kozol, Jonathan. 1991. *Savage Inequalities: Children in America's Schools*. New York: Crown Publishers.

Lemann, Nicholas. January 1991. "A False Panacea." *The Atlantic*.

Lewis, Anne C. April 1991. "Beefing up Our Wimpy Words." *Phi Delta Kappan*.

Lieberman, David. February 22, 1992. "Fake News." *TV Guide*.

Lockhart, William B., Yale Kamisar, and Jesse H. Choper. 1970. *The American Constitution: Cases and Materials*. St. Paul, Minn.: West Publishing.

McClenaghan, William A. 1990. *Magruder's American Government*. Needham Heights, Mass.: Prentice Hall.

Maddaus, J. 1988. "Parents' Perceptions of the Moral Environment in Choosing Their Children's Schools." Paper presented at annual meeting of the Association for Moral Education, Pittsburgh, Pa.

Mann, D. Spring 1974. "Public Understanding and Education Decision-making." *Educational Administration Quarterly*.

Miller, Julie A. October 9, 1991. "Report Questioning 'Crisis' in Education Triggers an Uproar." *Education Week.*

————. January 22, 1992a. "Fierce Partisan Fight on Education Looms in Congress." *Education Week.*

————. January 29, 1992b. "Senate Rejects Private-School Choice Proposal." *Education Week.*

Minnesota Business Partnership. 1990–91. *Resource Book.*

Minnesota Education Laws, vol. 1, Chapters 111–125. 1991. St. Paul, Minn.: Minnesota's Bookstore.

Minnesota Legislative Manual. 1991–92.

Mitchell, Emily. October 14, 1991. "Do The Poor Deserve Bad Schools?" *Time.*

Montano, Jessie. 1989. "Choice Comes to Minnesota." In *Public Schools by Choice*, edited by Joe Nathan. St. Paul, Minn.: Institute for Learning and Teaching.

Moore, D. R., and S. Davenport. 1990. "School Choice: The New Improved Sorting Machine." In *Choice in Education: Potential and Problems*, edited by W. L. Boy and H. J. Walberg. Berkeley, Calif.: McCutchan.

Mossberger, Irv. May 7, 1992a. "Recruiting Could Increase in Prep Ranks." *Duluth News-Tribune.*

————. May 23, 1992b. "Virginia Coach Censured for Recruiting Role." *Duluth News-Tribune.*

Mueller, Van D. 1991. "Financing School Choice." In *Financing School Choice.* Oak Brook, Ill.: North Central Regional Educational Laboratory.

Nathan, Joe. 1983. *Free to Teach.* New York: Pilgrim Press.

————. December 1989a. "Helping All Children, Empowering All Educators: Another View of School Choice." *Phi Delta Kappan.*

————. ed. 1989b. *Public Schools By Choice: Expanding Opportunities for Parents, Students, and Teachers.* St. Paul, Minn.: Institute for Learning and Teaching.

Nathan, Joe, and Wayne Jennings. 1990. *Access to Opportunity.* Minneapolis, Minn.: Humphrey Institute of the University of Minnesota.

Olson, Lynn. August 1990. "Prescription for a Revolution." *Teacher Magazine.*

————. September 18, 1991a. "Calif. Businessman's Drive for Choice Sparking Battle." *Education Week.*

————. September 25, 1991b. "Kozol Book Puts Human Face on Fiscal Inequities." *Education Week.*

————. November 6, 1991c. "Making Changes to Win Over Critics, Californians File Initiative on Choice." *Education Week.*

————. December 4, 1991d. "Milwaukee Voucher Plan Found Not to 'Skim' Cream." *Education Week.*

————. January 15, 1992a. " 'Supply Side' Reform or Voucher? Charter-School Concept Takes Hold." *Education Week.*

————. February 19, 1992b. " 'Entrepreneurial Spirit' is the Key to Reviving School, Book Argues." *Education Week.*

Ornstein, Allan C. October 1990. "How Big Should Schools and Districts Be?" *The Education Digest.*

Pipho, Chris. May 1991a. "On Becoming An Education Governor." *Phi Delta Kappan.*

————. October 1991b. "The Vouchers are Coming!" *Phi Delta Kappan.*

————. December 1991c. "School Reform: Critical Mass or Critical Mess." *Phi Delta Kappan.*

Publisher's Weekly. September 27, 1991. Front cover.

Randall, Ruth E., and Keith Geiger. 1991. *School Choice: Issues and Answers.* Bloomington, Ind.: National Educational Service.

Raywid, Mary Anne. 1989. "The Mounting Case for Schools of Choice." In *Public Schools by Choice*, edited by Joe Nathan. St. Paul, Minn.: Institute for Learning and Teaching.

Roberts, Steven V., and Gary Cohen. October 1, 1990. "Villains of the S & L Crisis." *U.S. News & World Report.*

Rotberg, Iris C. December 1990. "I Never Promised You First Place." *Phi Delta Kappan.*

Rothman, Robert. November 14, 1990. "Paper Launches Academic Attack on Chubb-Moe Book on Education." *Education Week.*

————. October 2, 1991. "1st Goals Report Contains Failures and Incompletes." *Education Week.*

Saint Paul Pioneer Press. December 22, 1991. "New School of Thought."

Schmidt, Peter. November 27, 1991. "School-Building Inventory Finds 1 in 8 Inadequate." *Education Week.*

Shapiro, Walter. September 16, 1991. "Tough Choices." *Time.*

Sheffer, Martin S. Summer 1991. "Presidential Power and Limited Government." *Presidential Studies Quarterly.*

Smetanka, Mary Jane. November 30, 1989. "Education Department Was Ready for Change." *Minneapolis Star Tribune.*

————. May 6, 1991. "To Match School With Child, Know Both Well." *Minneapolis Star Tribune.*

Time. December 12, 1985. "Let's Make A Deal."

————. September 16, 1991. "Not-So-Hidden Persuaders."

————. December 16, 1991. "Grounded for Good."

Underwood, Julie. October 1991. "The Financial Toll of Choice." *The School Administrator.*

Urahn, Susan. February 1990. *Open Enrollment Study: Students and District Participation 1989–90, Working Paper #1.* St. Paul, Minn.: Minnesota House of Representatives.

————. January 1991a. *Open Enrollment Study: Survey of School District Superintendents 1989–90, Working Paper #2.* St. Paul, Minn.: Minnesota House of Representatives.

————. March 1991b. *Open Enrollment Study: Patterns of Student Transfer 1989–90, Working Paper #3.* St. Paul, Minn.: Minnesota House of Representatives.

Viadero, Debra. December 4, 1991. "Pennsylvania Senate Approves Sweeping School-Choice Plan." *Education Week.*

————. January 15, 1992. "Experts Uncertain About Impact of Disabilities Act on Schools." *Education Week.*

Weinberg, Harry C. February 12, 1992. "For School Choice, Let's Follow the F.A.A." *Education Week.*

Weisman, Jonathan. September 18, 1991. "In Indiana, Business Groups Not Talking as One on Reform." *Education Week.*

Wells, Amy Stuart. 1991. *The Sociology of School Choice: A Study of Black Students' Participation In A Voluntary Transfer Plan.* Ph.D. dissertation, Columbia University.

Wisconsin Policy Research Institute. September 18, 1991. "Report Calls for Overhaul of Wis. Education Department." *Education Week.*

Wolcott, Lisa. January 1990. "The Diploma-Mill Scam." *Teacher.*

Wolken, Lawrence, and Janet Glocker. 1988. *Invitation to Economics.* Glenview, Ill.: Scott, Foresman.

Index

ABOUT THE AUTHOR

JUDITH PEARSON has twenty-three years of experience as a public school educator in Minnesota, the first state to experiment with choice in education. She has a Specialists' Degree in School Administration and holds Minnesota licensure for Secondary Principal and Superintendent of Schools. She has taught for thirteen years in secondary social studies; her service in administration includes seven years as Principal and two years as Superintendent of Schools.